"WITNESS OF THE UNKNOWN

WILLIAM JEVNING

ISBN: 10:154499382X
ISBN-13:978-1544993829

DEDICATION

To all the brave witnesses that have come forward with what they experienced. This first volume of "Witness of the unknown" is a collection of accounts sent to me by the actual witnesses who experienced the events they related to me. I have only done minor editing as to preserve the "flavor" of each witness as they told of the events they experienced. I have included six accounts that have been around for some time as a comparison for the reader to see how common many of the things happen from one witness to the next. There are many who have not come forward with things that they have experienced, my hope is that the accounts contained here and in future volumes will help them cope with events they endured.

WILLIAM JEVNING

1 THE COWMAN OF COPALIS BEACH

In the mid 1960's, my dad owned a large roofing product mill in Aberdeen, WA. He had teams of men that would cut the fallen old growth cedar salvage left after a logging operation. He had permits to salvage a large amount of wood in the coastal areas of Grays Harbor County, primarily in the area around Copalis Beach. Several of the men on his cutting crews lived in and around Copalis Beach. His foreman, a man I will call Jon for the story, was a bright, down to earth hard worker. My dad trusted him with thousands of dollars of vehicles and equipment, as well as the safety of his crews. He was not the kind of man to make up stories.

On a Monday morning sometime in July, Jon was several hours late for work. This was highly unusual as he was always there early, getting the saws and trucks ready for the day. My dad said he was visibly shaken up, and when he asked him what was wrong, he asked my dad to go in the office so the others wouldn't hear them. They went in and sat down, and Jon simply said "Something destroyed our house this weekend." My dad thought he said "someone" broke into the house, and asked Jon if it was someone he knew. Jon said, "You don't understand, this wasn't a person. It was a… I don't know what it was, but it completely trashed the house. The family is going to stay with my brother in Elma for a while."

My dad asked him to explain what had happened. Jon said that when he got home from work Friday evening, his youngest son Tim, who was around four at the time, told him he saw a big "Cowman" walking at the edge of their field that afternoon. He thought the boy meant "Cowboy", because some of his neighbors wore cowboy hats when they were out in the sun. He asked him if the man was wearing a cowboy hat, and the boy said, "No daddy, he was a Cowman, furry and stinky like the cows." He asked his wife if she knew what he was talking about, and she said Tim was playing on the porch that afternoon, when he came running in and said the cowman was stuck on the fence. He was very excited, so she went out to see what he was talking about. She said as she opened the door, she was hit by a horrible smell, like wet dogs and garbage. Tim was pointing across to the field opposite their house and said, "He got loose!" She looked where he was gesturing and could see the top strand of barb wire bouncing up and down, as if somebody had just pulled on it really hard and let it go. She didn't see the "Cowman", and noticed nothing out of the ordinary except for the smell.

She told Tim to come inside to play for rest of the day, she felt uneasy and a little scared. Their older son, Jon Jr. who was twelve at the time, was at a friend's house and walked home a short while after Tim saw his "Cowman". He told her somebody had followed him home, walking in the woods off the right side of the road. He never seen who it was, they never left the woods, but he said it had to be a really big man. He would hear large sticks cracking, and the footsteps were very heavy. Once he got to the driveway of their house where the woods stopped at the field where his brother had his sighting, the footsteps stopped and Jon Jr. never saw anything. He was pretty shaken up by the event, and wanted his Dad to go out to the woods and check it out with him.

Later that evening, Jon strapped on his .357 and took his older son out into the field to have a look. They first walked to the area where the "Cowman" was supposedly stuck on the fence, and walked down the fence line looking for anything. They came upon a large clump of long, reddish brown hair tangled in the top strand of barbed wire. He tried to pull it off but it was really tangled up, so he pulled out his buck knife and sawed it off. He said the hair was over a foot long, real coarse and stringy. There appeared to be a bit of flesh matted in the clump, and the top wire was pulled loose from one of the posts. Whatever was hung up on the fence was very big. He handed the hair to his son to hold, and they climbed through the fence and walked toward the woods. He said he was looking for any sign of tracks on the ground; the hair kind of looked like it was from a horse's mane or tail. The ground was a solid grassy field, and there were no hoof prints or any other tracks he could see.

The edge of the woods began about ten feet from the fence line, and they entered on a small game trail that deer frequented. It was around eight at night, and in the woods it was getting to be fairly dark. They walked for a ways, and soon began to smell the rotting garbage/wet dog odor his wife reported earlier. Jon said he got the feeling they were being watched; the hair on the back of his neck was standing up. He told his son they should head back before it got dark, and the boy didn't argue. As they began walking back out, they could hear heavy footsteps off to their left. They stopped, and the footsteps stopped. They walked on nearly to the clearing, and Jon whispered to his son to run like Hell to the house on the count of three. Jon Jr. nodded, and Jon whispered, "One, two...Three!" and gave his son a push in the back to get him started, then spun around and raced off the trail in the opposite direction, toward the footsteps with his gun drawn.

Off the trail, the underbrush was dense with ferns and bushes; he had a hard time making headway. But as he got closer, he could hear it moving away from him, deeper into the woods. At this time, he told my Dad that he thought it was a vagrant camping out in the woods and possibly scoping houses out to rob at night. Jon was a big man and capable of taking care of himself in most any situation and he had a large caliber handgun so he wasn't too worried about confronting a vagrant in the woods. He was a few yards off the trail in deep brush when he heard the movement stop just ahead of him. He stopped to look and listen, and thought he saw movement by a large tree, like someone was trying to hide there. He leveled his gun and said "Come out nice and slow, or I swear to God I'll come back there and shoot you!"

It was silent for a moment, and then he caught movement out the corner of his eye and spun around to his right for a better look. He said it looked like a huge bear moving through the brush, he could only see bits of it through the dense ferns, but it was moving quietly away from the tree on four legs. It was about fifteen feet away from him. At first he thought it was a bear, and then suddenly he saw a huge hairy arm with a human like hand reach out of the brush and grab a small alder tree. The tree was about four inches in diameter, and it grabbed hold about five feet up. He said it happened so fast it was a blur, but the thing pulled itself upright out of the brush by holding the tree. It stood on two legs and turned its upper body to glare at Jon. It was enormous; he couldn't believe how bulky it was. He said it was well over seven feet tall, and at least half that big through the chest. It was too dark to make out many features, but its eyes seemed to glow a deep red, and he thought he could see teeth, like it was curling its lips back.

It stood for just a brief moment, and then lunged ahead, pushing back on the tree with tremendous force. The tree snapped loudly and crashed into the trees around it, getting hung up in the branches and not falling to the ground. It then disappeared into the deep brush with frightening speed, sounding like a bulldozer with no engine sounds. Jon stood there in shock, his gun temporally forgotten, and then he realized it was heading toward the house, the way his son had gone. He turned and ran to the trail, hoping to gain ground on it and cut it off before it reached the clearing. He hit the trail and ran as fast as he could toward the clearing, all the while hearing the creature thrash through the brush on his side.

He burst into the clearing and looked franticly about for his son. Jon Jr. was standing just inside of the fenced field, waiting for his Dad. Jon screamed at him to run to the house, then he saw the thing crash out of the woods about fifty feet to his left. It crossed the ten foot clearing and stepped over the fence in two strides, and was running through the field parallel to his son in a matter of seconds. Jon screamed at his son to run faster, and took aim at the creature. He didn't fire because he was afraid to hit his son or his house, so he vaulted over the fence and ran in pursuit of them. He could see it angling toward his son, and knew there was no way his boy would make it to the gate before it cut him off. In desperation, he pointed the gun to the ground at his side and fired as he ran, hoping to scare it. It veered more sharply toward his son, and put on an enormous burst of speed. He heard his boy scream as they seemed to collide, he saw the creature dip its shoulder down a little bit and suddenly Jon Jr. was airborne, he flew about ten feet then hit the ground rolling.

The creature never paused; it continued to run at an amazing speed in a loop back towards the woods. Once the line of fire was clear, Jon stopped and squeezed off the remaining five rounds at the retreating creature. He was pretty sure all the shots went wild; the creature never made a sound or

slowed down, and was soon over the fence and back in the woods. He reached his son, who was shaken up but not physically hurt. He asked his Dad
if it was a bear. Apparently, little Jon was so busy running for the house that he didn't see the creature running after him, he said something big and black suddenly ran into him, and he felt a huge paw hit his bottom and he said he felt like he was falling.

Jon pulled his son to his feet and they ran through the gate and into the house locking the door behind him. They were both out of breath and white as ghosts, his wife was screaming at him, demanding to know what the gunshots were for and if they were all right. When he could catch his breath, he told her to make sure the back door was locked, he was going to call the Sheriff. He went to the phone and began to dial the number; this was before 911, then stopped and wondered what exactly he was going to say. He hung up the phone, realizing what an idiot he would look like if he told the Sheriff the boogie man just chased them out of the woods.

He told his wife that it was a large animal, possibly a bear. He didn't know how to begin to tell her their four year old was right, his Cowman was real and it was more frightening than anything he could imagine. He told them all to keep the doors locked, and stay away from the windows. Around ten o'clock that night, both boys were in bed and Jon and his wife sat down to watch the news. They soon heard a loud moaning cry, kind of like the siren on the volunteer fire department. It would stretch out for a long time, and then end with a "whoop whoop" sound. It was coming from the woods opposite the house.

His wife asked "What the Hell is that?"
Jon answered truthfully; "That is Tim's Cowman."

He then described to her the full details of what had happened, and she immediately wanted to call the Sheriff. He persuaded her that they would sound crazy, and that he would handle it himself. She reluctantly agreed, and told him she didn't want either of the kids to go outside until this thing was gone. The howling went on until around midnight, when it got quiet again. Jon wanted to stay up through the night and watch over the house, but he had a long day at work and the excitement earlier had worn him out. They went to bed around one in the morning, and had no further problems that night.

They slept in that morning, and the boys were already up and watching cartoons when they got out of bed. The first thing little Jon said was that he had heard the bear rubbing against the house last night. He said he was too scared to get up and tell his parents, and fell back asleep soon after.

Then Tim said "The Cowman talks funny."
This stopped Jon cold. He asked his son "When did you talk to the Cowman?"
Tim replied "Last night, in my room." Jon asked: "The Cowman was in your room?"

"No Daddy, he's too big for my room, he talked to my window." Tim said, and turned back to the cartoons. "What did the Cowman say, Tim?" Jon asked.

"He talks funny; I don't know what he said. He talks like this...OOH AHH AHH OOH!" Tim said, and started making strange monkey like noises. "Did the Cowman try to get in your window?" Jon asked, breaking out in a cold sweat.

"He's too big for that. He made funny faces, he has Lincoln Log teeth!" Tim said with a smile.

Jon later learned Tim meant it had square teeth that looked the same size as the small blocks in a Lincoln log set. It apparently spent quite a while "talking" and making faces outside the boy's window. Tim said it lay down and went to sleep outside, and he could hear it snoring. Jon walked to his younger son's room, and cautiously peered out the window. No sleeping Cowman. Jon told the boys to get dressed; they were going to go visit their uncle in Elma for the day.

After his wife and kids left, he called one of the men from his crew, and asked him to come over. I'll call him Patrick, he was an ex-State patrolman and my Dad said he was kicked off the force because of his drinking problem. He was a good worker and never got drunk before dark, so Jon figured they would have most of the day to look for this thing. When Patrick arrived, Jon greeted him at the door and said, "Are you up for some hunting?" Seeing how it was not hunting season, Patrick told him he doesn't poach, and doesn't even want to know about it if

Jon did. Jon told him it wasn't deer he was after, and went on to explain the previous night's events. Patrick didn't really believe him, but could see he was sincere and still shook up. Jon had his pistol and a bolt action 30.06, Patrick had a .38 in his car and Jon loaned him a 12 gauge. They first circled the house looking for any signs of a nocturnal visitor.

At the back of the house, there was a spigot for the garden hose, and it always leaked. There was a patch of ground worn bare of grass under it, and it had turned to mud. In the center of the mud, there was a huge, clear imprint of what looked like a bare human foot. Jon said it was at least 18 inches long, and very wide. It was so clear that he got the feeling it was left there on purpose. They found no other prints around the house, and in places in the field and woods where a track could be made, the creature seemed to avoid them. Off to the side of the track in the mud were four straight lines about eight inches long. He said it looked like someone had raked their fingers through the mud. When they circled around the side of the house and got to Tim's window, they saw what it was for.

Above the top of the window, a good seven feet up, were four muddy streaks. And on the window itself were dozens of large, muddy fingerprints. The glass wasn't cracked or broken, just smeared with mud. By this time Patrick was fast becoming convinced something strange had indeed happened the night before.

Before going out into the woods, Jon wanted to feed the families pigs. They had two of them apparently fairly young weighing around 40 pounds each. The pig pen was about a hundred yards away from the house, behind an old barn. As they got closer Jon became concerned because they couldn't hear them making any noise. Usually they squealed like crazy when they knew food was near at hand, but this morning it was completely silent. They rounded the corner and the pen was empty. No sign of damage or struggle, the pigs were just gone. They searched the barn but found nothing out of place, so they decided to hit the woods and try to kill this thing.

They entered on the same trail Jon and Jon had used the day before, Jon showed Patrick the broken fence wire and told him again about the hair. It was a bright summer morning, and Jon was surprised at the difference from the previous evening. The night before had been still and silent, now the woods were alive with birds and small animals. He showed Patrick the broken tree, and they followed the creatures' trail and found several more trees and large branches twisted and broken. They could see large, faint impressions of footprints where the ground was soft. They followed the deer trail further into the woods, and encountered nothing unusual. By noon they were both getting hungry, so they hiked back to the house for lunch. They spent the rest of the day poking around, but saw nothing more out of the ordinary.

Just before dark that night, his wife and kids drove up. He and Patrick were sitting on the porch with the guns, watching the woods. His wife asked if they had seen anything, Jon told her about the footprint and mud on the window.

Patrick had retrieved a pint of booze from his car and was well on his way to getting smashed. Jon decided he didn't want a frightened drunk with a gun around his family, so he suggested that Patrick could go home, nothing was going to happen anyway. Patrick agreed and drove off, and Jon continued to watch the woods. His wife brought out a plate of food and a Coleman lantern and a flashlight. He told her he would stay out here and watch the house through the night. Before they went to bed, he went into their bedroom and with help from his wife, pushed the king sized bed as far from the windows as they could. They agreed that his wife and kids would all sleep in that bed for the night and he would keep watch around the house. She had grown up hunting and knew how to handle a gun as good as him, so she insisted on keeping the shotgun in the room with them. He agreed after making her promise to ask for a name before shooting anything. If it replied "Jon", please don't shoot it.

There was a full moon that night, and Jon could see across the field and into the inky dark of the woods. The night air was filled with the sound of thousands of crickets, and the pond behind the house was full of croaking frogs. As the moon rose higher, clumps of weeds in the field began casting sinister shadows, and before long Jon was seeing big hairy creatures sneaking up on him in each of them. He stood up and lit a cigarette, trying to shake the fear and concentrate on the task at hand. As he smoked, he wandered to the end of the porch, and stood looking at the darkened barn. Something was different, but he couldn't quite place it. The front of the barn facing the house was open, and the moonlight was hitting it from the side, casting the interior in deep shadows. He stood watching the black opening as he finished his smoke, thinking about the missing pigs. He then realized what was wrong. All the crickets and frogs had gone silent. It was as quiet as the inside of a mausoleum at night; he could hear the minute shrill buzz of his own nervous system. As he turned to walk back to his chair, he thought he saw movement in the barn. He looked intently at the opening and could make out nothing, then turned his head a bit to the side and saw what looked like two red eyes hovering about eight feet off the ground. He couldn't see them if he looked straight at them, but when he averted his eyes a little, they became clearer. They were a deep burning coal red, almost invisible in the dark. Every few seconds they would disappear when the creature blinked.

His heart began thudding in his chest, and he waited for it to leave the barn and approach the house. He slowly backed up to his chair, never looking away, and picked up his 30.06. He walked back to the end of the porch and watched and waited. He stood looking at the blinking red eyes for what seemed like hours, and then the eyes blinked out and never came back. He watched intently but could see no movement. He thought for a moment, then grabbed the flashlight and shined it at the barn. The flashlight was too small to penetrate the darkness of the barn from this distance, he had to get closer. He was none too keen about leaving the relative safety of the porch and confronting a glowing eyed monster in his barn, but he was damned if he was going to live in fear in his own house.

He left the porch and began slowly working his way toward the barn, taking his time, building his courage up. He got closer and could still see no movement; it had gone further into the dark. He got within 20 feet of the opening, and his flashlight would now penetrate the gloom in the barn. He moved the feeble beam of light over the contents of the barn, an old tractor, and old pickup, boxes and buckets. Too many places for something to hide, even something big. He cautiously walked closer, now shining the flashlight down the barrel of his rifle. He stopped at the entrance and shined the light all over, searching the corners and under the vehicles. He stepped into the barn, every sense straining for sound or movement. He walked around the pickup, tensing for a huge, hairy arm to reach out and grab him at any second. He made his way clear to the rear of the barn without seeing anything, and slowly turned around to leave. He felt both relieved not to have encountered it in the dark barn, and frightened and somewhat confused about where it could have gone.

As he was walking out he glanced at the wide stairs leading up into the hayloft and froze. He knew with complete certainty that it had climbed those stairs and was waiting for him to walk out under the hayloft and jump down upon him. He couldn't move, he was literally frozen in fear. He swore he could here the floorboards softly creak above him as an enormous weight edged stealthily closer to the edge. He stood with his heart pounding in his ears, unable to move or act. Suddenly there was the booming explosion of a shotgun from the house, followed by his wife screaming. His paralysis broke and he bolted out of the barn toward the house, completely forgetting what may have been in the hayloft.

As he ran toward the house, he heard an inhuman roar coming from the woods behind the house. It sounded pissed off and in pain. It screamed again and he heard branches breaking as it plowed through the forest, thankfully away from the house. He got to the house and almost knocked down the front door in his hurry to get inside.

He ran down the hall to their room and found his family huddled together on the bed, sobbing. One of the windows was blown out, and his wife was still pointing the shotgun at it. When he burst into the room she swung the gun in his direction and screamed and he hit the floor. He waited for the blast but it didn't come. He slowly stood up and she had put the gun down and he went to the bed. He asked her what had happened, but she was too shook up to answer just then. Tim started crying:

"Why did you shoot the Cowman Mommy, why?" Jon Jr. Had his face buried against her shoulder crying. After they calmed down a bit, he told them to get up and follow him. He led them to the living room, then went out the open front door and looked carefully around. He could see no sign of it, all was quiet again. He told them to come out and get in the car. They ran out in their pajamas and piled in the car; he got in and drove them to his brother's house in Elma.

On the way there, they had calmed down enough to tell him what happened. She said a couple hours after they went to bed, she finally dozed off. She was awakened by Tim talking to someone, and this bizarre clicking chirping sound. Tim wasn't in the bed; he was standing in front of one of the windows. The moonlight was shining through both windows illuminating the room pretty good, but there was a large shadow, like a tree obscuring the window in front of Tim. She knew there were no trees close enough to cast a shadow, she told to get away from the window. "Mommy, listen! The Cowman can sound like a bird!" Tim said pointing excitedly at the dark figure in the window. "Timmy, get away from the window." She said, trying to keep her voice quiet. Right after she spoke, the noises from outside changed, it went from a soft chirping, to a strange gibbering, almost like human speech with an occasional pig-like snort thrown in.

At this time, little Jon woke up and said "What is that?" rather loudly. This seemed to incite the creature and it hit the side of the house with its fists hard enough for the walls to tremble. At this, Little Jon screamed and Tim yelled "Quiet, you're going to scare him away!" She yelled at Tim to get away from the window again, and reached up on the headboard and grabbed the shotgun. She got out of the bed and started toward Tim; the creature leaned down and looked straight in the window at her. She screamed and raised the shotgun, afraid to shoot because her son was so close to it. She started forward to grab Tim, and there was an explosion of breaking glass; a gigantic hairy arm reached through the window toward her son. She screamed again and fired over Tim's head, blowing out the rest of the window and hitting the creature with .00 buckshot. It jerked backwards out of the window and disappeared into the dark. A few seconds later she heard it screaming in the woods. "It was trying to get Tim, it was trying to grab my baby!" she started crying again and he comforted her as best he could while driving.

They stayed the rest of that night and the following night with his brother's family. He told his brother about it, but could see he didn't really believe him. He agreed to ride back to Jon's house with him early Monday morning before work. They had left the front door open in their haste to leave, and he was afraid animals or vandals would have got into the house. When they arrived, the house looked like a tornado had gone through it. The couch was upside down. They had a large, heavy console TV and it was apparently thrown across the room, lying in a spray of broken glass. The kitchen was trashed, the refrigerator knocked over and food everywhere.

The doors to both of the boy's rooms were left closed, and the rooms were untouched, same as the bathroom. The master bedroom was torn apart, the pillows ripped up and feathers everywhere. The chest of drawers was knocked over and the large mirror smashed. Jon's brother looked around in awe, and said "You better call the police!" Jon looked at him and said "And tell them what? Bigfoot destroyed my house?"

They left and closed the front door this time, and drove to my Dad's mill in Aberdeen. Jon's brother waited in the car while Jon went in and told this to my Dad. After he was done, my Dad said, "Well, let's go have a look at it then." They drove back out to the house, and Jon showed my Dad the damage. He pulled the clump of hair from his shirt pocket and let my Dad look at it. As they were walking through the house surveying the damage, my Dad pointed out cracks in the ceiling where it had apparently stood up and hit its head. Jon told my Dad that they couldn't live there anymore, even if the creature was gone, they would always be afraid. Their homeowners insurance wouldn't cover the damage; the adjuster claimed Jon must have done it in a drunken rage. My Dad helped them find a place in Aberdeen, and gave him a loan for new furniture and stuff. The house was eventually fixed up and sold, and my Dad never heard about another problem there.

A few observations about this story; My Dad lost contact with "Jon" and his family in the mid-eighties. They moved out of state and my Dad hasn't heard from them since. His brother died around the same time. Why didn't they call the cops? Jon had a lot of pride as well as a lot of common sense. He knew he couldn't logically explain what had happened to the authorities, and he didn't want the story to get out and have him branded a nutcase. I asked my Dad if they saved the hair, he said Jon never mentioned it again and my Dad never asked him about it. I asked my Dad if he saw the footprint and muddy fingerprints, he said he did. He said it looked like a giant barefoot man had stepped very carefully in the center of the mud. He's not a tracker, but he said it was the clearest print of any kind he had ever seen. I asked my Dad if the neighbors had heard any of this. He said if they did, none of them ever mentioned it again. I also asked him if he thought it was possible Jon had made it all up. That he HAD trashed his house in a drunken rage, and made up this elaborate cover story. My Dad said Jon and his family were terrified of that place; they didn't even want to go back and get their clothes.

If was just an elaborate story, what did he stand to gain? To profit from a story in any way, you have to share it with people. My Dad and the other folks mentioned in the story are the only ones who ever heard it, until now, of course. He also said that whatever trashed that house was no man. The TV had to have weighed close to 200 pounds, and it was obviously thrown across the room with great force. He said that even after two days, there was still a wild animal smell in the house.

2 AIR FORCE ENCOUNTER

I was born and raised in San Francisco Ca. in 1951. At an early age I became interested in UFO's, Bigfoot, etc. Read most of the early books by Ivan T. Sanderson and witnessed the release of the Patty film.

At about the age of 16 I began treks into the Mendocino National Forest North of San Francisco. I would spend days alone camped out and during the day I would attempt to find Foot.

At 19 and during the Viet Nam war I joined the USAF and was placed in the Security Police. In 1981 I joined the San Francisco Police Department and worked out of the Narcotics Unit. I have since retired (thank God)

I now live about a half hour north of Sacramento and only a few minutes away from the Tahoe National Forest where we do a lot of Gold Prospecting. Actually they do the prospecting and I'm checking for signs of Foot along the river banks and adjoining areas...........ha-ha

In 1971 after completing boot camp and specialist training I was shipped off to my first base at Davis Monthan outside Tucson Arizona. At the time it was a SAC (Strategic Air Command) Base with a couple of wings of B-52's parked in ready alert on the flight lines. Their job (if you saw Dr. Strangelove) was to penetrate Russian territory and bomb their cities. It was a very tight base and Security was everywhere of course.

On this base at the time, and I know they still have it. Was the Aircraft Boneyard where they had stored thousands of decommissioned aircraft that they would use for parts.

While working a graveyard shift with another Security Policeman we were asked by the guys working the entry control point to the Weapons Storage Area to bring out a few cups of coffee. We got them the coffee and began driving out to the storage area. The Weapons Storage area is where they stored the nuclear bombs that were used for the B-52's it was an area of 10 acres or so with bunkers spaced every few yards. The area was surrounded by fencing, concertina wire; light posts every few feet and an entry control point consisting of a small building near the entry gates. The building is manned by the Security division of the Security Police and they also utilized K-9 since this was such a sensitive area.

To get to this are from the base we had to drive down a two land road. On both sides of the road was the Aircraft Graveyard. Chain link fence lined both sides of the road. Every few hundred yards there were gates that were locked allowing entry into the boneyard.

The drive was maybe a mile or perhaps a mile and a half.

It was approx. 2 am when we drove down this road and delivered the coffee. Naturally there was no other traffic out there. We spend May 5 minutes talking to the guys who worked the entry point and then we turned around and left proceeding down the same route we took to arrive.

A couple minutes into the drive and directly in the center of the road we saw an object. At first we thought it was a car. As we got closer we realized it wasn't a car and upon inspection we were shocked to see that it was a propeller engine from a wind of one of the aircraft. It was missing the propeller but was about the size of a Volkswagen. We looked for drag marks but could find none. We also discovered that there were no entry gates nearby. It appeared that this engine that must have weighed at least a ton and apparently was taken from the boneyard area, transported over the fence and placed in the center of the road.

We called for our boss or the Flight Chief who arrived and after scratching his head several times with a whole lot of "what the hells" called for his higher up....

We were told to get back in our car. For the next couple of hours we watched as various high brass showed up including the Base Commander who we could observe examining the engine and general area.

Our Flight Chief then told us he would meet us back at operations and to wait for him. We did so and met him back at the office. He told us we were to mention this to no one and to forget it ever happened.

As time went on and I came to know the Security guys (Security Police back then was divided into two categories, Law Enforcement (which I was) and Security. Law Enforcement was like your town cop, whereas Security was the guys who guarded the aircraft on the flight line, storage areas, etc.) On base and they began to relate stories to me.

I was informed that many times in the Weapons Storage areas they would observed something very large, bi-pedal, and very fast in and about the storage area, when they would try and bring the dogs in the dogs would refuse and often try and pull away. These are Sentry Dogs!!!! These aren't your normal guard dogs!!! But they would refuse. They would see this thing usually running from light pole to light pole and it was something that occurred quite regularly. The "thing" could never be located.

I was then sent to Japan and after my tour there was given orders to my next base which was Luke AFB just outside Phoenix Az.

After about a year at Luke I was given the job of Desk Sgt. I worked various shifts mostly nights. After hours all calls from citizens wanting to report UFO's came to my desk and I would have to inform them that USAF no longer investigated (Project Blue Book) UFO's and would advise them to call their local Police Departments............ha !!!   I had of course read about the run a round that people got but I was now a participant in it. The calls came in quite often and many times I would ask for a relief from the desk and a few of us would go out and attempt to spot these UFO's

One night while working the desk, it was during the summer of 1974 (not sure of month), and I would say about 2am in the morning the SAT Team came into the office. SAT is an acronym for Security Alert Team. This is the Security Division of the Security Police as I explained above. The SAT team was a mobile unit made up of 2-3 Security personnel armed with M-16's They were a quick mobile alert team from any type of incursion on the base.

On this night there were 3 of them. They would come into the office quite regularly and get some coffee, stand around and B.S.

So they come in this night and they are very quiet. They get their coffee and just stand around saying nothing. They all got this look on their faces like they had just seen a ghost...........so I'm sitting there watching them and I finally tell them "Ok, what happened to you guys?" They looked at me like a deer in the headlights and one walks over and says "you won't believe what just happened to us"

Ok, tell me. So they say they were parked out on the flight line with the Dodge Six Pack vehicle shut off. 2 of them are in the front seat and 1 is in the back. They are sitting there relaxing and shooting the shit. This is a very open area and the flight line at that time (they have since improved it with high security fences) was in of course a desert area with no fences, just flight line and beyond it desert.

The passenger in the front seat is turned around and talking to the guy in the back seat when he sees this very tall black thing come running toward their truck from the desert. They said this thing was running at a full sprint. The guys in the front seat screamed to the driver to start the truck and get out of there. All three looked toward the "thing" as it approached the truck. The driver got the truck started just as this thing took a bounding jump and jumped over the rear bed of the Dodge. All three watched as it ran off at an angle into the desert. They then departed the area at top speed.

Very tall and very dark, humanoid shaped was their description of this "thing", and of course very fast!!!!

Fast forward again a few months. I'm sitting on the desk once again around 1-2 am when I begin getting all kinds of calls from civilians in the area that UFO's are all over the Phoenix area. I once again give them the brushoff. I'm telling some guys I work with what I'm getting, and since they too are interested in UFO's I decide to get relieved off the desk for a half hour and a bunch of us grab cars and go out to the flight line and point our vehicles toward the White Tanks Mountains in the distance. We were sitting there in maybe 5 different cars when the guy in the car to my right screams "what the hell is that" pointing out into the desert. We all hit our high beams and could see this tall black thing maybe 100 yards away. It appeared this thing was in a slow run or jog. We all started our cars and drove to exactly where it should have been, but nothing was there. How it got away or eluded us is unknown, it should not have been able to get away, and there was nowhere to hide!!!! I was now convinced that the SAT team had seen exactly what they say they did.

This started with a family deer hunting trip in the fall of 1966 by myself, my father Harry, mother Lola, and our pet dog Suzi. We lived in a suburb of Salem, Oregon called Keizer, and were traveling to an area southeast of Bend, Oregon called China Hat Butte in the Deschutes National Forest. The trip was to have lasted 5 days, but got cut short due to some serious Bigfoot events. During the 2nd night in camp we heard a noise like NFL Linebackers crashing through the trees surrounding the camp, brush being kicked into, and small logs being thrown about. Our pet dog was frightened in a life or death manner. This lasted around an hour it seemed like. Then around 2 hours later my dad got up and left the tent to use the restroom (friendly bush). He came back after what seemed like a half-hour frightened in a way I'd never seen him like. He was beet-red in the face, and was breathing hard. He then made an announcement that we were returning home the next morning, and said that we were going to tell friends that hunters were shooting too close to camp. We tried to get some sleep, and left first thing in the morning. After we picked up some ice cream cones in Sisters, my dad made another announcement, "I will never return to China Hat Butte as long as I live".

Time to move this report around 10 months into the future, in the early fall of 1967. My dad had started a secret letter-writing exchange with his fraternal twin sister Gladys. I knew of the letter writing, but my mother Lola had no clue. He would post the letters privately, without my mother's knowledge. Eventually he sort of slipped up on security a bit, and I was able to see partially the content of one of the letters. My dad was talking about getting the "D" brothers and sisters together for some sort of reunion, although I didn't know what that meant at the time. I was able to see other parts of letters (sent once per week). Eventually a near complete story came out in my 10 year-old mind. The "D" brothers and sisters (Brother Charles, Sisters Hazel, and Gladys) would gather in the fall of 1968 at the vacation cabin in LA Pine, Oregon owned by Brother Charles and wife Edna during deer season. They were going to use the Deer Season 1968 as cover to kill a big creature, or something, a beast? Bigfoot was not in the family lingo at the time. Let's back up and give you a feel for these family members. They were pioneering ranchers who settled the Fort Rock Valley of Northern Lake County, Oregon. They were trained as expert firearms persons from very little kids by a family connected to the Old West and Wyatt Earp's political machine. My dad was the best shot, so guess who would have been the main shooter on this trip? At Thanksgiving of 1967 my dad took his brother aside and brought him into the fold, I saw them both walk up the street after dinner to have a private conversation. The letters then indicated a planning meeting to be held at a motel in Bend, Oregon in early March of 1968. Then my dad started getting weaker physically as work became more demanding. By late September of 1968 my father suffered an aneurism of the descending aorta relating to heavy smoking. Then died about 10 days later. But while he lay dying in the hospital, some strange events occurred. I knew the storage place for the letter exchange file my dad kept, amongst his rock hound educational books and pamphlets, BUT my mother had no knowledge of them. Then one day I was walking to school while my dad was in the hospital, and parked near our house, around the corner, and out of sight from the house was a Ford Falcon Station Wagon with US Forest Service markings and paint. No one was inside. When I returned home and checked the letter collection stash file, the letters were gone. All I've ever thought is that the Law Enforcement arm of the USFS broke into our home and took the letters. All without any warrant presented to our family! How would they have found the location? One way, only one way, and that was to bully a man laying dying in a hospital, my father Harry! After the death of my dad, the private contract postal station in our suburb of Keizer treated my mother and me very rudely! Was there a USFS Law Enforcement intercept of our mail going on?

4 ASHFORD

My first incident with a creature I could not explain was in the summer of 1966. Our family traveled south down the Oregon coast. We crossed over into California, and Dad drove down past Crescent City. We drove back inland towards I-5. There were five of us in the car, Dad, Mom, my older brother who was 16, myself, then 15, and my younger brother, who was 13. We spent the night in Dunsmuir California. The place we stayed in had small cabins, and was west of I-5. I do not know the name of the place. There were several cabins, maybe 10 to 12 of them, and a caregiver/operators home. The people working there were a couple in their late 40's. They had three large dogs that were a Shepard mix. The dogs were very friendly, as my brothers and I played with them, throwing a tennis ball. It got dark early due to the thick forest and trees in the area. About two am, I awoke to the sounds of dogs whining. The dogs were chained up at the house of the caretakers. A mercury vapor light was lighting up the area between the house, and our cabin. I believed the distance to be about 60 yards. I could see the dogs by the porch area of the house, they were whimpering, and huddled together. I could see they were afraid, and looking out near an outbuilding or garage, I looked towards were they were looking, and saw in the street area a huge hair covered creature walking. It was at least 8 foot tall, and had long arms; it was just strolling on the small street, then into the woods. I was stunned, I did not know what it was, and I went back to bed, but did not sleep the rest of the night. Next morning the caretaker said something spooked his dogs, as they refused to leave the house after he fed the in the morning. I knew nothing of Bigfoot, and did not want today anything about what I had seen. The next year, my parents bought property in Ashford, in Echo Valley. We spent lots of time up there. Dad had a small 16 foot trailer, and the kids slept in a large tent. We saw elk, and deer walk through our property all the time. We would also see them in the meadow area, where there we several apple trees. The elk would pick them off the tree, and the deer seemed to feed off whatever dropped from the tree. In the late 70's we heard weird howling from across the Nisqually River. One night we heard a very loud scream from down by the river. It sounded like a high pitched woman screech. Next morning several people in the place commented about the screams. I by then I had heard of Bigfoot, and I believed that was what I saw in California. I was down at the river once collecting rocks to circle the fire pit, and I heard grunting from across the river. I left right away, not bothering to take the rocks. In about 1982 a large group of our friends were camping on the property in an old army tent. My younger brother was sleeping next to the tent sidewall. His girlfriend was next to him, and several others were in the tent. He was startled awake, when a large hairy hand reached under the sidewall and grabbed his arm. He yelled, and everyone was awakened. He was so shook up; he armed himself, built up the fire, and locked himself in his truck. He was in his late twenties at the time, and was out of the army. After that I only went there on day trips, and never camped there again. I know that there are Bigfoot creatures, I have heard them, seen them, and smelled them. I don't hunt or fish, or go on my own up in the area unless I am armed. Talk to the people in Echo Valley, and ask them what they have heard or seen.

5 HUNTING IN MINNESOTA

My name is Bob and I live in Minnesota. In October of 2008 I had an experience while out bow hunting for white tailed deer. What I experienced, I could only hear, I never saw what was making the noise. The noise alone scared the life out of me and I carried an AR-15 while bow hunting the rest of the year. I don't know if it was a Sasquatch or even if they live in this area.

This occurred in early October of 2008 while bow hunting about 20 miles south of Wadena, Minnesota. I had chosen a section of field that requires about a half mile hike to reach it because nobody ever really goes back there, and when I had I found a heavily used game trail. About 40 years ago this field was used for grain and corn but now is fallow and only used for hay on occasion. I was hunting the north end of the field which is only about 70-80 yards across but extends for several hundred yards to the south.

The temperature was in the low 60's and it had been beautiful and sunny all day. I was in a tree stand facing west and saw a buck enter the field from the western wood line and begin making its way across the field towards me. It was standing in some tall grass at 40 yards and I decided to shoot. I shot and almost immediately felt that I had missed (I flinched). The buck ran into the woods on the east side of the field and appeared uninjured. I have a personal policy of always searching for blood if I shoot at an animal to make sure I am being a responsible hunter and not leaving game in the field.

I climbed out of the tree stand just before dark. It was the time of dusk where the woods are too dark to see but you still have enough light to see in the fields. I was crouched down looking for blood/my arrow in the tall grass where I had shot at the buck. From the west of me I heard movement in the brush so i peeked through the tall grass and saw a larger buck enter the field. I knocked another arrow hoping for a shot, was facing west and had just taken a deep breath before drawing back my bow.

From the wood line directly behind me (about 40 yards away), I heard a sound I have never heard before. It started as an "Ooooohhhhhhh" and ended in an "Aaahhhh". The "oh" was deep and guttural and the "ah" was higher pitched and very shrill. What freaked me out was the volume. There is no possible way for me to make a noise as loud as this. I would say at minimum twice as loud as me screaming at the top of my lungs. I spun around and looked towards the wood line but the woods were already too dark to see into. When I heard the sound, I was instantly afraid (like a primal fear that you cannot control) and I had goose bumps on my neck.

The buck that had been on the field acted unusually when he heard this. Usually a deer will stop for a second, perceive a threat, flag his tail and run into cover. The second this scream occurred, this buck put his head down and bolted at top speed into the brush where no trail was. This freaked me out because now I was in the middle of a field with only grass for cover and some unseen screaming thing 40 yards away. I was now facing east again, looking towards where the sound had come from. I was trying to see any movement or hear any other sounds that could give away what this animal was. I still had an arrow knocked and I thought to myself that if this animal made the sound again, I would try to replicate it to draw it out onto the field where I could stick an arrow into it if I had to. I did not want to try a call after hearing only the first sound because it was such a shock to me, I was questioning if I had heard it right.

Then the shock of my life. As I was crouched, facing the wood line, the animal sounded off again. "OOOOHHHHAAAAAAAHHHHHHH!!!!!" The sound was clearly directed right at me and was so intense; I can barely put it into words. I remember that it was so loud that I closed my eyes because it was uncomfortable to feel a sound like that. It almost had percussion to it that felt like it roughed you up a bit. The sound it made sounded extremely aggressive and did not make me feel happy to be armed with only a bow. This really scared the crap out of me.

After a few seconds, I composed myself and tried to replicate what I had heard. The sound I made sounded like a pitiful whimper compared to what I heard and I did not even come close to matching the starting or finishing notes that this thing made. When I tried to replicate the sound, the animal immediately snorted/grunted at me. It was throaty, like how a hog snorts/grunts except I could tell that the sound was coming from about my own head height in the wood line. As it snorted it began moving away from me to the south, staying just inside the wood line. It was moving through the woods faster than I could run at a sprint. As it moved I could hear two things, the first was the

sound of brush clearing and branches breaking and the second was a very rhythmic thumping sound ... thump thump thump thump, which I took to be footfalls. I know the sound of deer hooves hitting the dirt and this was A TON louder than that, plus it was not in the same rhythm as deer hooves.
I could hear it breaking branches as it traveled inside the wood line for about 250 yards and then it got quiet as if it had stopped or was being stealthy. I got out of the woods very quickly at that point and felt pretty upset by the whole experience.

At the time of this event, I was finishing a college internship with the Minnesota Department of Natural Resources. I told the story to a Game Warden I knew and he jokingly said it was Bigfoot but then said i probably just heard a fox. I have tried to talk to a few people about this and everybody just pokes fun at me and asks if it was Bigfoot. The truth is, I don't know what it was and would really love some closure on that night.

This was absolutely not snort wheeze made by a deer.
This was not a coyote or wolf howling at me.
I have looked up fox calls and have not found what I heard that night. Also I don't think a fox makes noises 6' in the air and makes heavy footfalls.
This was not a cougar roar. (I ran into one on a different occasion and can firmly say this was not a cougar roar)
It screamed the loudest of any animal I have ever heard in the wild, hands down.
The buck was terrified.

The sound seemed to be coming from about head height.
It screamed and grunted and sounded aggressive.

6 NATIVE ENCOUNTER

I am 44 years old and I am a security officer for the Muckleshoot Indian Tribe. I have been a commercial fisherman for most of my life; I just recently started working a regular job. My first sighting was just a short encounter when I was probably 17 years old; myself and a few friends were sipping on a case of Rainier beer. We had just got the beer and I think we were on our first beer each. Our main spot for hanging out and drinking beer was a new building on our reservation just behind my house about 200 yards. There was a big front door area with a big awning over it; we used to hang out under. Just as we got relaxed and started joking and laughing, all of a sudden the dogs at the house nearest to us started freaking out and barking and growling. No one else was paying much attention to it, but it caught my attention and I moved out from under the awning and started looking toward the house where the dogs were barking. At first I didn't see much and suddenly I saw a slight movement out of the corner of my eye, and I saw a huge black figure peeking out from behind this green bushy tree that was kind of out in the open. At first I thought it was just my eyes playing tricks on me in the dark then it pulled itself back behind the tree!!!! I said out loud "HOLY SHIT!" and my friends didn't pay much attention to me and I told them I had just saw something peeking at me and they just laughed at me and kept talking. Just then it moved back out again and really quickly went back behind the tree.

It was then I realized how big this thing actually was, it must have been between 10 and 12 feet tall because this tree, although it was a young tree, was about 15 to 17 feet tall, and this thing went most of the way to the top of the tree. I told my buddies "hey man let's move out of here and go under the new big light pole they just put in down the street". They laughed and said no let's just stay here. I couldn't handle staying there after what I just saw so I told them "no man I'm serious let's go under the light". They still disagreed with me so I had to tell them that since I was the one who bought the beer that I was taking it with me to the big new light pole to sit and drink and if they wanted some of my beer they had to go with me. It was then that they realized how serious I really was, and they got real scared looks on their faces and said "oh shit, you are serious". I said I told you I'm not kidding around and I don't want to be here right now. We quickly packed up our beer and smokes and moved to the new light. We called our neighborhood god Woody to come and sit with nus because he was an awesome early warning system telling us when something wasn't right at night time.

The second sighting was a brief roadside sighting, me and my cousin were coming from a housing project which had a long dark road to get to the highway, and just as we were pulling out of the light it looked like someone tall was standing on the side of the road facing from our right to our left looking down at the ground, my cousin flipped on the bright lights and it looked up at us real quick. We got a real good look at this thing and it was a very scary moment because he looked right at us. We went right by him and we both looked at each other and said at the same time "DID YOU SEE THAT?" I don't know about him because he was driving but I got a real good look at this thing and it looked pretty scary!!! It was real stocky looking and had hair all over its body. It wasn't like most descriptions I hear about that say it didn't have hair on its face, it had hair on its face, its whole face was covered and I couldn't see any skin at all. The hair on the end of its arms by its hands was longer than the rest of the hair on its arms. Its eyes didn't shine in the light, I don't know if it was just the angle it was facing but I did not see any eye shine. The freaky thing was it didn't seem real big in comparison to a human; it seemed normal size which made us think maybe someone was playing a prank on us. We went back the next day to check out the spot where we saw this thing and to our surprise the trail on the side of the road where it was standing sloped down lower than the road about 3 to 4 feet below the road level, so this thing had to about 9 or 10 feet tall. This is the scary sighting that made me question whether I ever wanted to go into the woods again for about a year!!!!

I went hunting with my brother when I was about 24 or 25 years old and we brought his son, my nephew with us. We came up this road that was kind of steep, and when we got out of the thick timber there was a truck parked on the side of the road. After we went past this truck, the road kind of wrapped around this mountain curving to our left and above the road it was thick old growth timber and below the road was a very large clear cut that went all the way to the bottom of this valley where there must have been a creek because there were trees all along the bottom of the valley, then more clear cut on the other side of the valley. We went up and around this mountain and my brother said he would jump off right here and I'll go up over the top of the mountain and you drive back down the road and park on the corner and come up over the top of the mountain toward me and we will meet somewhere at the top. He said leave my nephew in the truck and lock the doors, my nephew was only 3 years old, but he knew how to wait in the truck because he always hunted with us. I was only going to   be away from the truck for 5 minutes tops. I locked my nephew in the truck and headed up towards the top of the mountain we were on. I got about 200 feet up in the thick woods and I walked up on a bow hunter in camouflage, I spotted him right off and I walked up to him quietly and asked him if he seen anything? He said he saw a couple does and that was all, he was a little perturbed that I was molesting his hunt, but I didn't do it on purpose. He got up and headed down the mountain and instead of going the rest of the way up the mountain I headed down also because he was going to have to go past pour truck where my nephew was. I got down to the road and started heading back to the truck, I could see it just down the road, so I stopped to check out the clearing just below the road. As I was scanning the clearing I thought I saw a big burnt stump just on this side of the trees at the bottom of the valley. I kept scanning and didn't pay it much attention. After

scanning the whole clearing, out of curiosity I
looked back at the burnt stump and it moved, at
first I thought it was a bear standing on its hind
legs but it never went back on all fours so I thought
"Ahhh I'm just seeing things", but I couldn't help
but pick up my 3 X 9 scope on my 300 Savage rifle,
that's when I got a good look at what I was
seeing!!!! I almost lost my breath and I started
shaking, I was looking at a giant!!! It was black, not
dark brown, it was black. It had hair from head to
toe and I could see its eyes, they were jet black
with no whites. Its hair was very long all over its
whole body, like real long, probably about 10 or 12
inches long like a guy in a guilly suit but there is no
man that big in this world. I know I was about 200
to 250 yards away but I could tell this thing was
massive. My first instinct was to run as fast as I
could down to the truck. I stepped back so it
couldn't see me and thought to myself calm down,
don't panic, and take a couple deep breaths and
just calm down. That's what I did, I took about 4
deep breaths and calmed down, I was still shaking
but I calmed down a lot. I then stepped back up to
the clearing and pulled up my scope, it was still
standing there, I was it looking around. Unlike most
descriptions I have heard it was turning its head
and looking around, it wasn't turning its whole
upper body it was turning its head like a person. I
started freaking out again and stepped back out of
sight, I wanted to run, and I wanted to just take off
as fast as I could to the truck but I talked myself
out of it once again. I slowly started walking toward
the truck making sure I was out of sight of this
creature. I stopped and walked up to the edge and

looked through the scope again. I could see everything about this creature, its hands, feet, arms, legs, and face. It was VERY VERY scary to look at its face!!! I realized that I had the cross hairs right between its eyes! But the thought didn't even cross my mind to pull the trigger, when I realized I was aiming at it I pulled the scope down and was looking at it with the naked eye then I realized there were 2 hunters just on the other side of the trees from it wearing blaze orange vests. I know they were farther away than this creature but they looked tiny compared to this thing, maybe half its size. I whispered to myself to get out of there you guys he's right there, then I looked through the scope again and the creature acted like he heard or sensed these guys were close by. He reached out with a hand just like a man's hand and grabbed a green leafed branch in front of him and let out a very high pitched scream like a woman getting killed, it was long and drawn out but towards the end of the scream it dropped into a low almost growl sound that scared the shit out of me, the hair on the back of my neck stood up and I once again felt like running!!!!!! I could see the 2 guys look at each other and to my relief started high tailing it away from the creature. Then I thought enough was enough and I walked briskly to the truck, my nephew unlocked the door and I jumped in and sat looking forward thinking about what just happened.

My brother came back pretty quickly and we left the area, I did not tell him what happened, I kept it to myself thinking he would call me crazy. I told a couple of my close friends later and word got to my brother. He pulled me off to the side at a family gathering and asked me if I saw something in the mountains. When I told him yes he got pissed, he told me "goddammit!!! When you see something in the woods you tell me right away!" I got real emotional and teared up and said I'm sorry bro, I just didn't think you or anyone would believe me. He said I'm your brother, you can tell me anything especially things like that, and I almost started crying and I'm not one to cry over just anything but what I was keeping inside me about this incident was eating me alive, and it was a relief to let it out to someone close to me like my older brother.

7 YOSEMITY FRIGHT

On Thanksgiving weekend of November 1989, I did a backpacking trip into Yosemite National Park. I was alone. My plan had been to take a 40-45 mile long trail that looped back to the trailhead that started near Hetch Hetchy Reservoir. This was supposed to be a three-day trip.

I got a late start out of San Francisco and arrived at the ranger station to check in at about 2:00. I told the ranger what my plans were and he told me, "You don't want to do that." I asked why and after attempting to sell me on another trail, he told me that there was a bear inhabiting the trail that was in my plan. It was following people, he said. But I was set on this plan; I told him I wanted to do it anyway. He told me to go ahead then, but to "keep my wits about (me)." It was a weird exchange. In hindsight, I wonder if he knew something he wasn't telling me.

I got to the trail at around 3:00. There were no other cars at the trailhead. With the sun setting in a little more than an hour, and with rain on the way, I start booking up the trail. I wanted to cover as much ground as I could. One thing I noticed right as soon as I entered the forest was that it was completely silent. Being from the East Coast and having never been in the Sierras late in the year, I told myself that it must be the normal state of things. It was unsettling. I worked my way up the switchback from the trailhead and the trail straightened out and went into a steady incline through a high-canopied forest that was relatively clear of underbrush. One could see a good distance on either side of the trail. I began to hear what I thought was something moving through the woods, paralleling me. Every time I stopped, the sound stopped. I told myself that my ears must have been playing tricks on me, because I would peer into the woods to find the source of the sound and I would see nothing. I must have stopped 20 times to look. That's how clearly I heard something above the white noise that I was making as I traversed the trail. And I needed to haul ass and couldn't afford to keep stopping. So finally I told myself it was nothing, tuned it out, and moved up the trail.

I must have covered about four miles before I stopped at a clearing by the trail to make camp. The sun was going down. Rain was beginning to fall. I quickly put up my tent. I put my food in a sack, threw a rope over a high branch, and hauled it up and tied it down. While I did that I had the sense that someone was staring at me. It was so powerful that I knew what direction it was coming from. Someone or something was staring a hole through my back. I turned around and peered into that direction and saw nothing. I looked for a good five minutes or so, time I really didn't have to spare. I never thought that an animal could give one that sense, but what else could it be? I told myself that it must be a deer. It was not a good feeling. The rain started coming down. I didn't build a fire. I collected some rocks to ward off any unwanted visitors. I went into the tent for the night.

This was a perfect night for sleeping. It was pitch black. There was no moonlight. There was no wind. The only sound was the gentle sound of a light rain falling into the forest. I didn't sleep at all. I was filled with dread. It was a feeling I couldn't rationalize and I was getting annoyed with myself. I thought I was being a head case. And I had an overwhelming sense that something was wrong and I was in trouble.

I had been lying awake for two or three hours when something hit the roof of the tent. It freaked me out. I sat up and I can't recall if I said it aloud, but I thought, "What the fuck?" My mind started racing. I started having a panicked conversation with myself. "Someone threw something at the tent." "That can't be. There's no one out there." "Then what the fuck happened?" "Something must have fallen from the tree. A pinecone." Then another projectile hit the tent. "It sounds like a pinecone." A third hit the tent. That's when I convinced myself that pinecones were failing out of the tree that I was camped under. I ruefully noted to myself that it was just my luck, in a night as weird as this one, to be camped under the only tree in the Sierras that was losing all of its cones that night. I don't know how many more fell on the tent. Maybe it was five or six? Once I rationalized what it was I tuned it out and focused on wrestling with the sense of doom that hung over me.

At some point later I head an animal approach the clearing. It was a welcome sound. Besides the phantom sounds paralleling me on the trail, it was the first living thing I had heard. I was listing for a bear and it certainly wasn't that. It was too big to be a skunk because it broke twigs under foot. I though it must be something in between: a raccoon. Then as it was crunching around, I thought, "That's one clumsy assed raccoon." Being tense and angry, I decided to take it out on the coon. I stuck my head out of the tent and yelled at it in the blackness. I gave it the what for. I threw rocks in the direction I thought it was. It seemed like a foolish over reaction. The animal did not make another sound. I didn't hear it move away. Strange. It's like it evaporated into the forest.

As dawn approached, I decided to abandon the trip. I wasn't having any fun. As soon as the sun came up, I got out, rolled up my sleeping bag, packed up the tent, got the food down, and headed back down the trail. I must have done all of that in less than five minutes. I have a vivid snapshot of the memory of noticing a small collection of pinecones next to the tent. I made note of the weirdness that they all seemed to fall in the same place. But that was just a flash of a thought and then I moved on to getting the hell out of there. I had an overwhelming sense that I was in danger. I had given into the fear. And I was disgusted with myself for feeling that way because there was nothing rational to pin it on. I hauled down that trail and I purposely tuned out everything around me. I finally saw my first living creature, a bird flying above, when parking lot first became visible through the trees.

This experience bothered me for years. I don't think of myself as someone who scares easily. I couldn't understand that fear. I never told anyone about it because it embarrassed me. I'm a levelheaded person and I regarded it as the weekend I became a head case. I never looked back and considered the things that had gone on. I just thought about my emotional reactions. Then I stopped thinking about it altogether.

8 CAMPING NIGHTMARE

Bud who was a deputy sheriff at the time and
patsy his wife went camping up near flaming gorge
on the Utah Wyoming boarder. There were no
other campers in the area. The first night was
 uneventful. On the second morning Patsy got up
before dark to go the bathroom as there camper
had no toilet. They had a port a potty set up close
to camp , when Patsy was finished she was tying up
the bag when she heard Low huff as she looked up
she swore she saw a head behind a tree , she
 noticed the long hair more than anything, so she
hurried back to the camper (it was almost a full
moon) . Patsy woke Bud up and told him she swore
there was a very tall homeless man watching her,
Bud chuckled and said Patsy we are miles from
anyone, Patsy told Bud that the man smelled awful.
Bud blew it off and they started there day as they
was leaving to go fishing the bag that Patsy had left
by the fire pit was now on the good of their truck,
Patsy advised Rick that she had placed the bag by
the fire pit, Bud was now a little suspicious but not
wanting to miss the early morning fishing they left.
They got home around 5 pm from the lake and
Patsy began preparing dinner , after dinner it was
just starting to get dark more like dusk , Bud was
lighting the lanterns when he heard a large tree 75
yards away crash to the ground, Bud told Patsy and
their son to go into the camper Bud follows them in

and took his .357 and returned outside, he walked over to the tree he noticed an odor and a huge set if barefoot tracks I guess this really made him nervous , Bud was a big man he stood 6.1 and weighed 260 and I compare him to John Wayne as he was feisty and didn't take any guff.   So he went back to tell Patsy that it was nothing, he didn't want to upset her. Later that night around 1 am there son woke them and said that something was brushing up against the camper I guess they was so tired they put the son in bed with them , 30 minutes or so they woke to a scream that went through there soul I'm told. Patsy said that is it let's get out of here, Bud took his pistol out with a lantern and found nothing.   To get through this story fast a few things were missing in camp like his lantern and his pole was broke the next morning - later that night was the worst night - approx. 11:30 just before midnight the camper shook violently this is unclear if the door was unlocked or if Bigfoot pried the door open but suddenly the door was open and there stood at least a 8 and a 1/2 foot creature - Patsy screamed and their son jumped off the lower bunk and ran toward them Bud fumbled for his pistol, a lot of commotion was happening Bud said - there son was crying and screaming for life Patsy was in the line of fire so no shot was fired. The Sasquatch just stared at them the huffed and left. They told my folks that time stood still but it was probably less than 2 minutes that Bigfoot was in there view. Bud did get to the door and he could here the Sasquatch crashing through the trees... The camper had to be welded and a new door frame had to be constructed. Very costly. Patsy swears that she heard these screams in her dreams for years and years... I personally over heard my parents talking to Bud and Patsy when we was camping in the Uintah's - we camped a lot and I was always scared to death because my bunk was close to the door, this story has stayed in my mind my entire life. Left out a few things to save time but there propane tank was smashed and   they found a large pile of pinecones on their picnic table one morning. Bud passed away last year - he made lieutenant before he retired from the sheriff's office. He got me hired on as a deputy when I was 21; I worked as a deputy for 5 years before taking a position at Delta airlines where I still work.

9 MICHIGAN ENCOUNTER

The first encounter was happened with my father when he was a child. I believe in was around 1977-1978 Barrington Michigan. My grandparents had gotten a small house and lived outside of town. My father was the middle child of five, two sisters and two brothers. They used a camper as a chicken coup and had a massive, and I mean massive guard dog. That dog, so I've been told, wasn't scared of anything or anybody. It had a large chain attached to the camper to protect the chickens. Anyways, this night my grandfather wasn't home, he was out at work driving his large eighteen wheeler. It was pitch black outside, and my father and his siblings were all in bed, and my grandmother was out in the living room. My uncle claims he felt something wasn't right, he just felt very, very scared. When out of nowhere, everyone smelled a horrible skunk like odor and the dog went berserk. The dog was barking up a storm and just went crazy. My grandmother said she believed there was a bear outside and didn't want to go outside, but the dog was acting extremely aggressive. Unnaturally so. About seven minutes or so after the dog had started barking, this massive, loud, bone shattering cry woke all the kids up and scared the life out of my grandmother. It's hard to describe this sound according to my father and his siblings it was like a semi roar, that was deep at first but got higher in pitch a sound no human could make, and it was very long, vocally speaking. The dog was so scared that it yelped and went under the camper.

There was a dead silence, but everyone allegedly heard the dog's chain being forced against the concrete/ground, as if being pulled out from under the camper. My uncle heard a loud commotion and got out of bed to go see what was going on, he claims he saw red eyes in the light looking at him and it scared him so bad that he instantly hid under the bed, my aunt and grandmother also saw red eyes in the light and it equally terrified them. The next morning, the family went outside to look around and what they saw really tore them up. The dog was gone, all that was left was the skin of its back and all of the chickens were gone too. The only way to get inside the coup though, was to go under the camper where the latch was, and the dog was in front of it, something crawled under the camper, forced open the latch and stole all of the chickens. No bear could have done that, no cougar could have done that, no wolf could have done that. There were feathers and massive feet print all around the house and area. The newspaper was called in and they actually took casts of the foot print. My father's family left after this and he wants to take me up to Barrington to see the casts one day. I personally believe it was a family group that attacked the house. Because my uncle, aunt and grandmother saw one staring at them all within seconds of each other, at different spots of the house. I think the house was surrounded, as well as multiple ones carrying off all the chickens and the dog.

 The next encounter that my family has, is a bit more sketchy and I'm not too sure if I believe it myself, but allegedly my uncle who was so terrified of the event, instinctively remembered the smell and just...the atmosphere kind of like a vibe in the air, like it wasn't abnormal. Well, he went hunting with some friends, I think the year was in the mid 90's or so...but anyways he was out hunting with his friends and he caught that same sent. His friends commented claiming they thought it was a skunk, he told them no it this was no skunk it was a Bigfoot and that they should leave. Well immediately all his friends started making fun of him and made him mad. So he told them, alright you just wait and see tomorrow morning something will come up. Well the next morning according to his story, some miles away, I think it was about 5 miles, something had carried a cow over a six foot fence and tore it open and took some organs out of it and left the carcass behind. Now, I've not been able to verify this myself, it was a long time ago sense he told me this event, but he swears up and down that it's true and he becomes rather angry if you act like he's lying.

 The last and final encounter, (that I am aware of at least) happened in the mid 2000's with two of my cousins. They actually took me to the spot where they saw it, and it terrified my cousins so much that they refuse to travel alone in the woods ever again. It was late at night, and my cousins were driving home, and the road passes through some pretty heavy forests, where they live in Michigan is pretty thick woodlands. And they passed this corner where there's this small little cemetery, with a single street light. Well they passed this corner and they both see this massive large figure standing right under the street light and they knew immediately what it was and it scared my cousin so bad, the one driving, that he actually fainted out of fear. This thing was massive, large, and hairy and gave off the vibe that it meant business. And my other cousin had to slam the breaks and stop the car. He said, he knew he had to get out of the car to put my other cousin (the driver) in the back so he could drive off, but it was almost in a state of panic, he didn't want to get out because he was overcome with sheer terror, an over-gripping amount of fear. They both say they've never been that scared in their lives, he thought if he got out of the car he was going to die. Well eventually the thing disappeared or left and he got out and switched seats and drove off, but neither of them will ever talk about it unless you ask them questions and refuse to go into the woods alone ever again.

10 THE VISITOR

Somewhere in the Eastern Sierras.   10,000 ft. Level

We left the trailhead about 12:30 p.m. We pretty much had a lake in mind where we wanted to camp. We packed enough for 3 days and two nights. We arrived at the lake about 3:30 p.m. There was a couple there just for the day talking pictures that they sell professionally. The gal tells my husband, Todd, there is an area off trail over this crest with a couple of lakes that not a lot of people know about. Well, that's all we had to hear, because we are all about remoteness! So we trek on over this ridge and down the other side...and now we are in a "bowl" of sorts and it is beautiful! There is a big lake and a little lake and there are "shelves" of granite all around the lakes. We saw one person fishing there and he had a tent set up on one of these shelves. So, we hike around and find a spot higher and a ways from where he is. Set up camp, and then we do the triangle thing where your camp is in one spot, your kitchen in another and your bear canister in another. We cooked dinner about 4:00 p.m. And then cleaned up. It had started to rain a little bit so we got ready and put everything, food and toiletries and anything that had a smell to it, in our bear-proof canister. Now the rain really kind of started to pick up so I get off all my rain gear and crawl in the tent. Now it is pouring and hailing so Todd just stands out here for a few minutes with his rain gear on and when the rain lightens up a little he takes his stuff off and crawls in the tent. We know we are in for a long night, because it is only 6:30 p.m. And we are already in the tent for the night!

At 12:30 a.m. I am woken up by the most hellacious noise I have ever heard. I am just absolutely startled and I wake Todd and tell him that a bear has got our canister...this noise goes on for a couple of minutes and it is VIOLENT! It sounds like the bear is taking the canister and slamming it over and over onto the boulders. We each have a bear spray and Todd has a handgun. I say, "Todd, chamber one in that thing!" He does and so there we are in our tent in the middle of the forest in the Sierras, in the pitch dark and all this is going on. I was terrified! Never felt anything like it in my life! We sit there not moving a muscle for about fifteen minutes and then we hear footsteps...one, two, three coming toward our tent and then silence. Right when it took the third step I said "here it comes!" Todd says, "I know, Jo you cannot panic!" It was the first time in almost 30 years that I saw my husband frightened. It went dead silent and we never heard it leave. I was just picturing this pissed off bear waiting for us in the dark outside our tent. About a half hour later, we hear something on the other side of the lake, just crashing through the forest. I never went to sleep and Todd dozed off and on a little, but we were both in our bags clutching our bear spray and Todd, the gun. I shook the whole night and did

everything thing I could not to throw up and also mess   myself!
Daylight finally arrived and Todd got up to go see the damage done to the canister...... It had not been touched or moved! The hair stood straight up on his arms and he said the words...Jo, I believe that was a Bigfoot! I am convinced. It was so angry   and   wanted   us   gone!

11 THE APEMEN OF MT. ST. HELENS

I wish to give an account of the attack and tell of the famous incident of July, 1924, when the "Hairy Apes" attacked our cabin. We had been prospecting for six years in the Mt. St. Helens and Lewis River area in Southwest Washington. We had, from time to time, come across large tracks by creek beds and springs. In 1924 I and four other miners were working our gold claim, the Vander White. It was two miles east of Mt. St. Helens near a deep canyon now named "Ape Canyon" — which was so named after an account of the incident reached the newspapers.

Hank, a great hunter and good woodsman, was always a little apprehensive after seeing the tracks. The tracks were large and we knew that no known animal could have made them: the largest measured nineteen inches long.

It was in the middle of July, and we had received a good assay on our claim, and everyone was excited. I remember I had a tooth that was aching, and I suggested to Hank that he should take me to town to see a dentist; but he was so enthused in the prospects of the gold mine, he barely took time to answer me. He replied that "God or the Devil" could not get him away from there. We had all come up in his Ford, and I had no way to get to town unless he took me. So when we went back to our cabin, on the north side of the canyon, I had a nagging tooth ache and little appetite for our evening meal of beans and hotcakes.

Hank, though apprehensive, was still determined. We had been hearing noises in the evening for about a week. We heard a shrill, peculiar whistling each evening. We would hear it coming from one ridge, and then hear an answering whistling from another ridge. We also heard a sound which I could best describe as a booming, thumping sound — just like something was hitting its self on its chest.

Hank asked me to accompany him to the spring; about a hundred yards from our cabin, to get some water, and suggested we take our rifles — to be on the safe side. We walked to the spring, and then, Hank yelled and raised his rifle, and at that instant, I saw it. It was a hairy creature, and he was about a hundred yards away, on the other side of a little canyon, standing by a pine tree. It dodged behind the tree, and poked its head out from the side of the tree. And at the same time, Hank shot. I could see the bark fly out from the tree from each of his three shots. Someone may say that that was quite a distance to see the bark fly, but I saw it. The creature I judged to have been about seven feet tall with blackish-brown hair. It disappeared from our view for a short time, but then we saw it, running fast and upright, about two hundred yards down the little canyon. I shot three times before it disappeared from view.

We took the water back to the cabin, and explained the affair to the rest of the party; and we all agreed, including Hank, to go home the next morning as it would be dark before we could get to the car. We agreed it would be unsound to be caught by darkness on the way out.

Nightfall found us in our pine-log cabin. We had built the cabin ourselves, and had made it very sturdy. It stood for years afterward, and was visited by many sight seers until a few years ago when it was burned to the ground — the circumstances of the fire, I do not recall.

In the cabin, we had a long bunk bed in which two could sleep, feet to feet — the rest of us sleeping on pine boughs on the floor. At one end of the cabin, we had a fireplace, fashioned out of rocks. There were no windows in the cabin. So darkness found all of us in the cabin, more calm now (and my tooth was better, somehow the excitement seemed to work a temporary cure on it). We were sitting around, puffing on pipes, and talking about the trip home the next day.

Each of us settled down in his crude, but welcomed bed, and soon fell asleep. About midnight, we were all awakened. Hank, who was sleeping on the floor was yelling and kicking. But the noise that had awakened us was a tremendous thud against the cabin wall. Some of the chinking had been knocked loose from between the logs and had fell across Hank's chest. He had his rifle in his hand and was waving it back and forth as he kicked and yelled.

(Hank always slept with his gun nearby — it was a Remington automatic, my gun being a 30-30 Winchester, which I still have).

I helped to get the chinking off him, and he jumped to his feet. Then, we heard a great commotion outside: it sounded like a great number of feet trampling and rattling over a pile of our unused shakes. We grabbed our guns. Hank squinted through the space left by the chinking. By actual count, we saw only three of the creatures together at one time, but it sounded like there were many more.

This was the start of the famous attack, of which so much has been written in Washington and Oregon papers throughout the years. Most accounts tell of giant boulders being hurled against the cabin, and say some even fell through the roof, but this was not quite the case. There were very few large rocks around in that area. It is true that many smaller ones were hurled at the cabin, but they did not break through the roof, but hit with a bang, and rolled off. Some did fall through the chimney of the fireplace. Some accounts state I was hit in the head by a rock and knocked unconscious. This is not true.

The only time we shot our guns that night was when the creatures were attacking our cabin. When they would quiet down for a few minutes, we would quit shooting. I told the rest of the party, that maybe if they saw we were only shooting when they attacked, they might realize we were only defending ourselves. We could have had clear shots at them through the opening left by the chinking had we chosen to shoot. We did shoot, however, when they climbed up on our roof. We shot round after round through the roof. We had to brace the hewed-logged door with a long pole taken from the bunk bed. The creatures were pushing against it and the whole door vibrated from the impact. We responded by firing many more rounds through the door. They pushed against the walls of the cabin as if trying to push the cabin over, but this was pretty much impossibility, as previously stated the cabin was a sturdy made building. Hank and I did most of the shooting — the rest of the party crowded to the far end of the cabin, guns in their hands. One had a pistol, which still is in my family's possession, the others clutched their rifles. They seemed stunned and incredulous.

The attack continued the remainder of the night, with only short intervals between. A most profound and frightening experience occurred when one of the creatures, being close to the cabin, reached an arm through the chinking space and seized one of our axes by the handle (a much written about incident and a true one). Before the thing could pull the axe out, I swiftly turned the head of the axe upright, so that it caught on the logs; and at the same time Hank shot, barely missing my hand.

The creature let go, and I pulled the handle back in, and put the axe in a safe place.

A humorous thing I well remember was Hank singing: "If you leave us alone, we'll leave you alone, and we'll all go home in the morning." He did not mean it to be humorous, for Hank was dead serious, and sang under the impression that the "Mountain Devils" as he called them, might understand and go away.

The attack ended just before daylight. Just as soon as we were sure it was light enough to see, we came cautiously out of the cabin.

It was not long before I saw one of the apelike creatures, standing about eighty yards away near the edge of Ape Canyon. I shot three times, and it toppled over the cliff, down into the gorge, some four hundred feet below.

Then Hank said that we should get out of there as soon as possible; and not bother to pack our supplies or equipment out; "After all," he said, "it's better to lose them, than our lives." We were all only too glad to agree. We brought out only that which we could get in our packsacks. We left about two hundred dollars in supplies, powder, and drilling equipment behind.

I tried to persuade everyone not to relate the happenings to anyone, and they agreed, but Hank soon let the cat out of the bag. We made our way to Spirit Lake, and Hank went in to the ranger station. He had told the ranger earlier about the tracks, and the ranger had replied, "Let me know if you find out what they are." That was just what Hank did, to the puzzlement of the ranger.

When we were back home in Kelso, Washington, he told some of his friends, and somehow the story leaked out to the papers, and the Great Hairy Ape Hunt of 1924 was on.

Local reporters interviewed us. They came from Portland and Seattle — even a big game hunter from England came asking questions, and he had a large gun with him that must have been an elephant gun. Many people flocked to the Mt. St. Helen's area looking for the "Great Hairy Apes", or "Mountain Devils." I, myself, went back with two reporters and a detective from Portland, Oregon. We found large tracks, and they photographed them. We did not see any of

12 OUTDOORSMAN

1974-1998: Lived in CA, MO, TX, NM, back to CA, and then OR. I'm a big nature freak - tons of hiking, fishing, camping, Nothing ever happened.

1998: Relocated to Springfield, MO, attending college. Was out in eastern OK (Adair County) with an old friend from OR who had relocated to Locust Grove, OK. We were driving around looking for salamanders, a hobby AND an academic pursuit for me. We had pulled over to check a creek out and parked my car. We walked perhaps 30-50 yards from the car, but around a small hill, following the creek, out of view of the car. We're in the creek, flipping rocks and looking for salamander larvae in the creek when we hear the distinct "ping" of rock hitting my car. Then again. I half yell "what the hell" in that direction, thinking its kids throwing rocks at my car. We weren't too far from some houses after all, and its scattered forest and pasture land. Then we hear a big bang - something big hitting my car. We walk back to my car and there's a rotten Osage orange right next to the driver's side door. There's still Osage orange on the spot where it hit. We can't see anything or anyone, which to me, is bizarre. Its early spring, not too thick, so I feel we should be able to see the culprit(s), but we can't. We get in my car and drive away to the north. As I'm driving, my friend looks back and says

"I see him!" At this point, I don't care. Throwing rocks at cars in rural Oklahoma is a good way to get shot or get yourself seriously hurt otherwise, so I figure if a person is willing to chuck rocks at my car, I want no part of that situation. As I drive on I ask what he looked like - was it a kid? And he says "It was a big guy, tall, wearing a black hoodie and black pants going straight up the hillside very fast. Almost hopping and using his arms to propel him up. Big dude for sure".
We never really spoke about it again.

2000-2002: This time period includes undergrad and graduate time, studying Eureka salamanders. My study site is Busiek State Forest, south of Springfield MO. My first task is to hike every creek and tributary in the park boundaries, to survey for the presence of the salamanders. In two particular ravines west of HWY 65, I get a very creepy feeling, the classic "being watched" but think little of it. Then east of HWY 65 in part of my survey, I follow Woods Fork as it goes north to the park boundary. Well, I can tell by the vegetation and the geology of the hill, that there's likely a spring/cave on the private land perhaps 100-200 yards away. So I hop the fence and head over there. Well, the first thing I run into at the vegetation spot of interest is a pile of bones. Its cows, deer, maybe some other stuff...all scattered around an area perhaps 10 x 10 feet under some trees. Nothing too fresh though, there's no hide left or anything like that. Weird to have it concentrated like that. But man, the creepy feeling is back, big time. I chalk it up trespassing! Sure enough, there's a very small cave with lots of nice salamander habitat. But I don't linger too long, because I'm just feeling paranoid for no good reason, it seems, so I leave.

Two days later. It's rained, and I know that spot I found will be even better now that the salamanders will be out and more detectable. So I head that way, but as I get to the spot where I hopped the fence - which is NOT a trail - there's a red tailed hawk carcass draped over the top strand of barbed wire, more or less exactly where I crossed two days prior. This stops me dead in my tracks. It's been dead a while, no head or internal organs left, dry and slightly mummified. The only place I EVER find hawk carcasses is on the road, which is a good three thousand feet away as the crow flies. No animal would have put it there - a raccoon would have easily just walked underneath the bottom strand with it, there would have been no need to try to climb over the fence with it. Why would a person put it there, off-trail like that? Would the landowner have done it? Why not put a sign instead telling me to stay off the land? This really bothered me. I remember standing there dumbfounded, knowing that hawk was a message for me alone to find.

The next spring, another buddy of mine from OR came out to visit and perhaps relocate. He was hoping to scout out a decent spot to camp, and I was interested in looking for salamanders, and we were bored...so at roughly 8pm-ish, we head to Busiek. It was definitely dark by the time we arrived. We park at the west lot, near the firing range. As we get out, I start to stroll across the bridge to the firing range while my friend heads off the opposite direction to relieve himself. I cross the bridge, noticing there's a couple tents out at the firing range, and begin the right turn to hit the trail going west. Suddenly I hear brush popping, rustling to my right - maybe 10 feet away. I immediately scan the area with my tiny LED flashlight, looking for the armadillos or raccoons responsible. I remember thinking armadillo, because that place is crawling with armadillos. Well, I can't see an armadillo, but the foliage is in motion, as if something was there but stepped back further, letting the vegetation close back after it. I'm puzzled. I see vegetation moving, but no critter. Then suddenly - this is the best I can describe it - a wall of vegetation perhaps 10 feet tall and 10 feet wide is moving/shaking violently all at once, but for the life of me, I cannot see what is making this happen. It's disorienting. Simultaneously, a feeling of dread like I'd never felt before hits me. It's stupendous. It must be what the deer feels like as the tiger leaps for its neck. No doubt about it, I have the unmistakable certainty that I'm about to be ripped to shreds and eaten. Or abducted. Or both. I can't overstate how powerful and unmistakable this feeling was.

Now this is completely irrational and over the top to the situation, in hindsight. I sort of went into a biological autopilot and began backing up on the path, stomping my feet and dragging them in an exaggerated fashion, as if to let whatever was in the bushes know I was there, I guess, and ready to fight. I can't really explain why I did it. Makes no sense. It seemed like an eternity to me, waiting for this thing to rush out of the bushes and grab me, but as I'm doing this I'm backing up to the bridge and meet my buddy, who's about halfway across. He asks me what the hell I'm doing, because I must have looked like an idiot, and I remember saying "Something just came at me in the woods! Something tried to snatch me!" which wasn't exactly true. But it was exactly how I felt. I was absolutely panicked and terrified, and I've been in the woods in the dark so many times...it just makes no sense. But anyway, as we stand on the bridge, we suddenly hear distinct bipedal footsteps in the chert gravel of the stream bed below. The creek was totally dry. And the gravel beds are chert and limestone, and very deep in spots. It makes a very distinct; almost ring/chime sound as you walk across them. Well whatever this thing was, it took 6 or 7 VERY heavy, plodding steps in this gravel bed and stepped across to the north and was gone - maybe just some faint sounds of vegetation moving as it went up the hillside north of Camp Creek. We strained to see anything from the bridge with my flashlight, but saw nothing. He said something like "well are you ready to hit the trail?" but I was done. We got back in my car and left, and I pretty much trembled the whole way back, with a weird sort of electrical "hair on end" feeling on my neck and arms.   Bizarre.

I've never been back to Busiek at night again.

13 LONG AGO

I tried to remember everything about what happened, I would appreciate you leaving out the families names and mine. I did forget that dad had told me, he thought they were probably after a calf. I only saw 1, but dad said there were at least 3 he could see. He also said when he was a boy they would steal meat from the smoke house. He had lost his father when he was 12; there were 6 kids and his mom living in a one room shack on the bank of the river. Well here is the first time I actually saw 1. It was 50 years ago this month.

My family raised cattle along the Sulphur river of East Texas where my father was raised he and my grandmother both told of wild men in the forest & swamps there. Ever since I was old enough to open gates and stand in the seat of a truck we would go down at night and feed hay, range cubes & corn meal to the herd we had. As I grew up, from around 11 I would go by myself with the family dog to carry out that task. One thing dad always hammered into my head was, never go without a gun and never be afraid to shoot and he would take care of the rest. I never saw what he called a wild man when I was alone. I did hear and see one when he was with me when I was about 7. It was a summer evening still light enough to see, but shadows crawled across the country road as we made our way to the gate, the farm/ranch was about 4 or 5 miles from a farm to market road. I wasn't really happy to be on this trip because I had gotten a mini bike for my birthday and this was burning up valuable riding time. It was 1965, I remember now because that is when I got that bike & a double barrel .410 shotgun. We survived off of the garden and what we could kill to eat, sometimes we bought groceries like milk, hoop cheese & things of that nature, sorry i strayed from the topic a bit, but I want you to understand we were country folk. My dad was an inspector at an army base 32 miles one way from our house and he drove a bus to make extra money carrying riders to and fro. And when he would get home around 5 we would eat and then go feed. This day he was running a bit behind schedule because he had had a flat on the old bus. Anyhow as we pulled up to the gate our dog was acting silly whimpering a half growl half spooked kind of way. Dad told me. Stay in the truck, which was unusual because opening gates and putting out hay was my job. Well he opened the gate and we had another 400 yards to get to the coral & an old sawmill that hadn't been used since the forties. As dad went to get back in the truck, he did an odd thing.....he slipped his 30-06 out of its case behind the seat and put his 12 gauge in the case behind the seat. He checked it for shells and had me hand him 3 more from the glove box, he then loaded the gun and chambered a shell without a word he put the gun between us and continued on. As we got up to the corral I noticed just about every cow we owned with the calves were either in there or trying to get in. We had mostly Hereford cows, our bull for that pasture though was a tame Santa Gertrudis we called bully we could call his name and he would come right to us. Dad was like that with most livestock. I didn't see bully at that moment and I turned to say something to dad and he was already outside the truck he had left the door open and our usually scared of nothing dog was out and under the truck. It scared me the way dad was acting and our dog to. Dad said to me come here and bring that box of shells with you. I did as I was told without question. Now that corral was about 200 yards from the tree line and the pasture around it made kind of a backwards L (this was the Henson Portion of our lease which joined the Old wommack place where my mom's relatives were raised and because most of the families had moved away dad leased it all and took care of all the issues of mailing lease payments to each heir.) We were in what would be the bottom of the backward L, in the angle stood an old timber forest it had been there since the depression. There was an old wagon road there that probably hadn't been used in 50 years. Between us and that road stood Bully rubbing his head in the dirt and throwing dirt high in the air, I thought he had gone nuts and dad was getting ready to shoot him, that was not the case though...It was just as I was turning back towards our beloved bull that I heard what could best be describe as a cross between a scream and a roar it shook me clean to the ground it almost seemed like the sound ran through my body. Our dog got back in the truck. My dad called me over to him, the light of the setting sun threw shadows across the meadow, I heard dad whisper there he is and pointed to a spot just north of the wagon road.......now back in those days I could see two gnats fornicating at 500 yards...but I couldn't see what dad was pointing at and then that scream came again and it stepped into the field, it made what seemed like only 4 strides and it was halfway to the old sawmill a good 200 yards across from where it walked out of the woods, it stopped there and turned toward us I didn't sense any fear in him, but I definitely felt fear, I it was still a good 100 yards away, I kept waiting to hear the report of dads' gun, but he didn't shoot. For what seemed an eternity it stood watching us and then in an instant it was gone. I looked at my dad and he said that is one of the wild men I told you about, that thing was huge, as he stood in the middle of the field, it looked as though his hand dropped past his knees, he didn't have really long hair but he was covered except for his mouth and eyes with hair... He was very stout looking, not a knotted muscle, just tough. I thought back on all the times I had been down there alone either working a fence line or feeding or riding my horse or bush hogging or cutting thistle from the meadow and all the times i had explored that old wagon road looking for what was left of the cabin where dad raised and climbed that old saw mill sawdust, memories that flood back even today. I didn't see another one until I was 17 in another county about 50 miles south from this site.....but that's another time in the fall of the year.

14 SUSAN'S ENCOUNTER

Here's my story of what happened to me back in 1971, I was eleven years old. I lived in Spanaway Washington a population then about 7,000 located in the outskirt of Tacoma. In the 40's the government came in and took a lot of property from residence to create the Military Reservations which is hundreds of miles big. The five acres behind our house borderline with the military reservation with a bob wire fence so there is lot of woods behind our house and all the other neighbors' houses for miles. Our neighbor had three older boys they raised and when they pasted on the boys got the house and property. They placed trailers on their back property and moved in with their new families. The very back lot one of the boys moved on had children so I began babysitting for them when I was about ten and there place sat very close to the reservation property. As kids we were always outdoors sleeping out all the time in the summer. I never heard no sounds from the reservation at all except for in the 60's there was a lot of military activity out there and sometimes I would hear a pack of dogs running through the woods barking as they ran. (People dumped their dogs out there all the time when they did not want them). We were not allowed to go out in the res. but of course we did we were just very careful about anyone seeing us. One Friday night I went next door to babysit in the house that sat on the back lot. They went to the bar and stayed until

2 am and then came home. The lady Chris always walked me to the fence line of our properties and from there i would run on down to my house. It was a very clear night, full moon and easy to see outside without a flashlight. So we headed out the door talking and laughing and proceeded to go to the fence. About halfway there we suddenly hear this animal and it just let out this long bellowing scream. We froze in our footsteps looking into each other's faces wondering what the hell it was. I was thinking whatever it is it was huge because of its blood curdling scream and it was very close to us although we could not see it. After it stopped I turned around and ran like hell back to her place and she was right behind me. Once we got in the house we woke up her husband who was passed out on the couch. He wouldn't get up so we called his brother who lived up front in the big house. (They had gone out with Chris and her husband to the bar). He came down with a loaded gun and walked me to my house. He then walked the perimeter and did not see anything and went home. Back in 1968 my neighbor had a birthday party and we went to the movies. They showed the short clip of big foot that Roger Patterson filmed so I was aware of the Big Foot but there was no sound with the clip. In 1972 a documentary came on called "In Search Of" with Leonard Nimoy. The very beginning of the show they play a loud long scream of a sasquatch and the hair raised on the back of my neck because that's exactly what I heard coming out of the woods. It was the only time I heard this in the 16 years I lived there but it was the day I believed in Bigfoot.

15 GEORGIA EXPERIENCE

Before these encounters I've never had any kind of experience with Sasquatch, I've only had the common knowledge about them from watching Unsolved Mysteries, In Search Of, and The History Channel, growing up. Truth be told, I only thought of Sasquatch being in the Northwest, never something I would encounter in South Georgia.

 My first encounter took place at my friend Matt & his little brother Hunter's cabin along the Alapaha River, east of Tifton, Georgia, and a bit north of Alapaha, Georgia (about 50 miles north of the Okefenokee Swamp area & Florida) in the late fall of 2010. The cabin is along a curve in the river where it makes an inverted T with the cabin sitting on the top of the T. It is way back along the river and is privately gated off along with about five other cabins. It sits way back in the woods with the nearest constantly lived in house about a mile away where the entrance gate is. Just a lot of old growth forest, planted pine forest, and a few farming community houses around fields, you barely see people at all back there.

Anyways, it was around 11PM and there was about 4 of us to begin with just hanging out, and cooking out at the cabin, trying to have a relaxing weekend. After a while, a few more friends call to say they were on their way. Because the area is gated off, someone has to drive down to the gate to unlock it to let them in. This ultimately becomes my friend Alan and my self's job since the other two guys with us have already had a bit too much to drink. So, when the first friend's car gets to the gate we tell them we'll be down to let them in.

I drive down and Alan gets out to open the gate while I sit in the car with the headlights on so he can see what he's doing. Now this gate sits beside the only non-vacation house in the area to the left and woods immediately to the right. The car pulls in and Alan is walking the gate close when I see him suddenly stop and his head snaps towards to wood line like he is staring at something. He hastily locks the chain and kind of jogs to the car. When he gets in I ask him what all that was about. He says he heard something grunt at him, and I ask like a dog growling? No, he says, it was real guttural and he tries to imitate it and asks if I heard it. I tell him no, I had the radio still going and write it off as a wild hog - which potentially being gored by one is still pretty scary if you run across one.

About 45 minutes to an hour passes and the last of our friends get to the gate after getting lost trying to find the place and Alan and me ride back down to let them in. By this time Alan is a bit unnerved and wanted me to get and unlock the gate with him to see if I hear any grunts, which I tell him that's not happening, but I would roll down the windows and shut the car off to listen. He unlocks the gate, let's them in, and the same thing happens, something grunts at him from the woods, but I hear it this time. It was no wild hog, it was way too deep and guttural to be and I could "feel" this grunt like a bass drum can be felt when it's hit. I yell out for Alan to hurry up as I turn the car back on and turn around. When he gets in we try to place that grunt, but it was nothing like we've ever heard. We end up just saying it was probably a bear, because there is no other animal that could grunt like that, but we both knew that was no bear. When we get back to the cabin we tell everyone to be careful and not go outside alone because there may be a black bear around.

A short time after that, Alan, another friend, and I step down to the dock that juts out off the bank into the river - which is about 15 feet below us. We have the dock light on and that casts light out across the river and a few feet up both sides of the opposite banks. We're out there talking and I'm casually tossing some rocks in the water as we talk. I don't know when I notice it, but I start to notice that when I toss a rock into the water, there's a few second pause from the splash and then there is another splash down the river a bit. This continues for a few moments when my other two friends notice my face is getting white and I'm staring across the river without saying anything. They ask what's up and I tell them something is throwing rocks in the river after I do and we all kind of stare as I throw another rock in. I notice on the left bank there is a shadow darker than the surrounding area beside one of the pine trees that is just beyond where the dock light reaches trying to stay still and it is tall, stopping just below the first limbs- I'd say at least 7 feet. This freaks me out a bit and finally I pick up a big hand of gravel and a pine cone and chunk it as far as I could to the left bank to see what happens. I'm thinking this is some homeless guy messing with us and I'll see him move when he throws back. This shadow stays still like its watching and there is a few moments pause after the rocks splash and down the river we hear this big KABOOSH sound like a boulder was thrown into the water. We decide this is enough for one night and go back into the cabin for the night, and lock up and keep all the outside lights on.

Shortly after this, Alan and I come to the conclusion that wasn't some guy messing with us. Alan lives about 7 to 10 miles away from the cabin in a small town between Tifton and Alapaha. When we first met he recounted a story to me about when he was about 8 or 9. One night his dad and he were watching TV downstairs in the living room while his mom, brother, and sister were asleep upstairs. At one point, they hear their Rottweiler in the back yard just start barking and growling. His dad gets up and grabs a flashlight and a shotgun and tells Alan to stay in the living room. When he gets into the kitchen and is about to head out the back door, he hears the dog struggle like it was fighting and whimpered suddenly and stops. Alan's dad opens the door and whatever was in the backyard just let's out this deafening bloodcurdling roar. He turns on the flashlight and all he sees is this black shadow shakes the bottom limbs of the trees as it hopped over the 6 foot fence and was gone. He found the remains of their dog at the foot of their pear tree beside the fence. He described it as if something had picked up their full grown Rottweiler and crushed it into a ball the size of a basketball. His dad got a sheet, wrapped the dog up, and put him on the kitchen table. Alan described his dad as the most frightened he has ever seen him, and he doesn't frighten easy. He locked and barricaded all the doors and windows in the living room and got the rest of Alan's family and made them sleep in the living room while his dad sat in his chair facing the door with his shotgun in his lap and stayed awake the whole night.

His grandmother told a story shortly after that about back in the 1960s when the area was still fields, woods, and dirt roads with very few houses, that she was driving near their house around dusk and this tall, slender, black thing burst out of the woods near a pond and began to chase her car down the road. She said it screamed like a woman and had red eyes. His family doesn't talk about it and for the longest time he called whatever this thing was the Banshee from that scream.

It wasn't till after our first encounter at the cabin and his dad telling him about how he and his uncle saw something like a Sasquatch near that part on the river back in the 70s while fishing at night that the pieces came together. After he told me his dad's encounter fishing I played some alleged Sasquatch sounds/screams and asked him if this is what he heard as a kid. When I played those sounds was the only time I have ever seen my friend genuinely terrified to the point of shaking and tears. He had me turn it off because it was just like what he heard and he couldn't listen to it anymore. That is when he became convinced that this was a flesh and blood animal we encountered.

The second encounter I had was also at the cabin in October of 2012. My friend Hunter, who wasn't with us when the first encounter happened, wanted to experience what we did and wanted to go out there one night. I told him I doubt it would ever happen again and that's probably a good thing since if these things are primates they aren't exactly giving out hugs when they become territorial. He still wanted to go however and so we and three other friends, including Alan again, went out to the cabin. I kind of wish we hadn't.

We sat out on the dock with all the lights off except the porch light and decided to tell stories to pass the time, because honestly, I never expected to have another encounter in my life. About an hour and a half passes and we hear this low growl/whine come from near the neighbor's newly built cabin. We don't think anything of it, thinking it the neighbor's dog or something. Except, my friend Emily points out that the dog is huddled under our back porch stairs. We ignore it and stay out on the dock.

As we take turns telling stories, I notice that there sounds like an animal is moving down the bank on the opposite side of the river to my right. I reposition my chair so I wouldn't have my back to the noise. About 25 minutes after the growl sound, it's my turn to tell a story. Emily goes inside to take a phone call and I begin my story. Not long after beginning I notice that I don't hear any forest sounds, no birds, no frogs, no crickets, just silence. About the time that I notice this, we hear what sounds like a wolf howl roughly 75 yards away from where I heard an animal approaching, and this thing is loud, and not coyote like at all. This scares the living hell out of everyone and we get up to the porch. My friend Jarod and I try to remain calm and listen to the forest, but I can feel this overwhelming sense of dread and panic begin to wash over me. Especially when I realize there are no wolves in Georgia.

We stay on the porch and try to listen to see if we hear anything, and Jarod crosses over from being calm to what I consider stupid as he goes back down to the dock and tries to knock on a nearby tree to see if he can get something to knock back. I try to get him to knock it off and explain to him at the same time that primates knock on trees when they're territorial and that's some bad mixed signals he's throwing out. As he's walking back to the porch we hear this call that is hard to explain. It sounded like a wounded turkey, but off somehow, I'm not sure how to describe it, and it was coming exactly from the spot that the wolf howl came from. We're like what the hell is that, because of the same location of the calls just a few moments apart. It sounds again but towards the end it morphs into something like a mix between a gorilla and chimpanzee "hoot call".

When I hear that, panic sets in. We hear limbs snapping and banging across the river and suddenly the motion detector light on the side of the neighbor's cabin comes on and the chickens he had in a coop start going crazy. You can hear something circling the back of our cabin through the pine forest as well and it's. Jarod is still on the dock and I'm convinced I'm about to watch my friend die. All the while, my brain is straining to comprehend how this thing got from one side of the river to the other without hearing it wade or swim the river and up a 15 foot sheer bank face to set off the motion detector in a matter of seconds. That added a new level of fear to the memory.

Eventually the sounds died off after a few hours, but that feeling of being watched and dread still lingered till daylight and so did the eerily silence of the forest. We kept trying to figure out what had happened, a few try to rationalize that it could've been some escaped chimpanzees, but you could tell they didn't believe that themselves. The following morning we looked around to see if we could find any tracks, but the forest floor was too hard packed and covered in leaves to see any, but you could tell something had moved through that was big from how disturbed the leaves on the ground were.

 After that, I haven't really been back to the cabin. Later on, after doing some research, I found that folks have been having encounters all along the Alapaha River in surrounding counties. Though, I still have lingering doubts about what I encountered since I never actually saw one, and I'm kind of glad

I didn't. For years I've had nightmares about these things and the cabin, breaking in, and killing my friends. Long before ever hearing about the more aggressive stories. It's like a primal anxiousness that's like muscle memory or something with encountering these animals. I know that it has robbed me of my comfort of a lot of outdoors that I enjoy and as interesting as the whole topic may be, I regret knowing these things roam around.

16 INDELICATE ENCOUNTER

Both of these ladies grew up in the woods- one as a logger family member in Oregon; the other in another western state. They both told me accounts they'd heard of going way back in their families! I was shocked, to say the least.

Makes me wonder, if all the witnesses of these creatures told 2 of their friends of their accounts, how many would open up and relate a tale of their own? The magnitude would likely astound us.

So the one (under total anonymity) has told me privately this account. She started by saying she was at the place and time when it happened, just wasn't a participant.

It was on a vacation trip to Colorado in the 70's when she was a teen; with a number of relatives, a small family reunion campout thing. I don't know where in CO but near Boulder is all I heard. Her older cousins all from that area, (18-24 yr. olds-2 males 1 female) were going to explore a cave or old mine shaft they'd found earlier in the campout and wanted her to go along. She is a sheepish individual and I have a hard time picturing her even going along to see this cave. But she did and after 2 or more hrs. Heavy hiking- more of a scramble- up a rocky mountain side they saw a dark opening above their heads. After getting everyone up on the ledge that was in front of the entrance they ate and drank tons of water and she supposes their campsite was at 5,000' and this had to be at around 6500 or more. It was clear and crisp out and windy as it usually was, she said. She was used to the altitude and 3 cousins also but remaining member cousin was not, and was having trouble with exhaustion, nausea and thirst. She had no interest in entering said cave/mine so stayed outside with that cousin. The 2 males and 1 female entered cave squatted nearly to their knees to enter. She was outside with another female exhausted family member.

After a hr. they were well rested and getting sunburned- so she called into the cave and although she got a slight echo of her voice no answer came back. They decided they were getting too burned by wind and sun so wrote a message in the dirt saying they headed down to tree shade area.

Going down was worse than climbing up so it took and hr. to get down to the shaded areas and they thought they'd heard the others coming down a ways behind them. Expecting the rest of the troupe, as they sat under the pines in the shade, drinking the last of their water- she hollered out, "I hope you haven't used up all your water because we need more!"

No answer came. But they definitely heard scrambling around in the rocks up above them but couldn't see up there due to the scrub and trees they'd entered. After a few minutes she hollered back again saying they weren't going to scare them as they could clearly hear them coming down the hillside, so just come straight down and quit messing with them.

All noises halted. She and her companion had to pee but didn't want to go as they were sure they'd get caught with their pants down...literally!

Nature dictated they were going to have to risk it, so she went around a boulder and the other kept watch for the wily cousins. After she came out the other went behind the boulder. As she stood looking up to try and discern their arrival, she saw something huge, and black moving around in between openings in the brush.

She said she instinctively knew it was too big for her cousins and then her brain tried to make it into 2 maybe or maybe even all 3 huddled together- but even so she thought it would have been more like 5 of her cousins wide (all 3 were skinny as bean poles she said).

She got an eerie feeling and when her partner came back from the bathroom boulder she suggested they head back towards camp as she thought there may be a bear up there. They made a lot of noise and singing as the worked their way down hill (rather steep at this section) and it switched back a little at a point so she stopped and looked up and back and saw the big boulder they used- now seeing it from the backside- the side they had urinated on. All at once, a big brownish black "rock" at the base of the boulder moved....bobbed up and down a bit she said. Her partner also saw it move and though they were quite a ways from it- it looked to be bent over and at that it was almost to the top 1/3 of the boulder. She said having gone behind it they both knew it was at least 3' above their heads when standing - and thought it was around a 9-10' tall rock.

It kept bent, bobbing to and fro close to the rock then back; when they heard the others from up above calling to them. With that sound of their voices the animal "perked up" she said and they then clearly saw a head and shoulders instead of rounded shape- and then it exited stage right- she said. She could never see the base of boulder or creature just head and shoulders- and it simply moved right and gone!

She tried hollering up to companions but the wind carried her voice off- and when she saw them next they were at the tree area they had stopped to rest at.

They babbled their sighting to them; then heard their account. They had entered the cave; found it to be crude mine from a long ago time. It had remnants of wood scrap and cans, and junk. It seemed to go back about 200' or so but they only went in about 100' as it narrowed so much it was crawl on your belly time after that. They looked for historical items, clues to what had been mined etc. and just rested. It wasn't very dark inside as it had air vents (seemed like natural holes) that let light in. After 1/2 an hr. or so, they had a whiff of urine so strong they said it'd make your eyes burn...then it was gone. They supposed that animals had used the area as a latrine. So once in a while this acrid smell would waft out to them as the rummaged around the junk left by miners.

Nothing was worth retrieving so the girl had thought she'd a least take an old can as a souvenir, and they scrambled back out; said it took a good 40 minutes. Just to get in and to turn around another 40. They stayed inside a good hour or more they thought. So exiting cave they saw the message in the dirt and started to go downhill. They thought they heard the 2 ahead of them so they were thinking they'd catch up to them in a few minutes, but when they heard one of them call from far below they stopped.

They couldn't discern what was said but it did not sound urgent so they resumed. Suddenly the female of the group smelled the acrid urine again! The others didn't but she was sickened by it, actually. The guys stopped and nosed the air and one said he caught skunk cabbage odor- one caught a whiff of musk and other nothing. So thinking it may be a bear they too made noise as they eased forward.

When they got to the edge of pines where the other 2 had stopped to rest and go behind the boulder, they heard some "Hmm? Grr..." sounds! They all 3 immediately went to ground they said! It was such a powerful voice they knew it wasn't human- so crouching by the pines they listened as something behind the big boulder made odd vocal sounds ...when it made to leave as the ones at bottom of the hill saw it go to rt. - these guys saw it exit from behind the rock going to their left and said it was a cross between a bear and a gorilla or something. None saw the face but all said it was at least 8' tall slightly bent forward and had arms to its knees which were bare like the hair had been worn away from crawling! It was gone in a flash. They sat awhile and then eased toward the boulder (had to go around it to get down the hill she said) and they paused only seconds to look at area the creature had been standing in. Saw nothing but did see the wet dirt and noticed it had been piled up into a small hill against the boulder. They did not know it was urine wet soil at this time.

When the group all was on the same page they

were wondering what the thing was doing with the urine-pile. Said no bears would do such a thing.

After arriving at the camp 2 of them told some of their folks and all agreed it had to be a bear. My friend, however, said she knew all her life that it was not.

17 EASTERN EUROPEAN ENCOUNTER

Let me start by saying when this experience occurred I had no knowledge of the Sasquatch Subject and to be honest I didn't believe, during the early 2000.s up to 2008 we experienced An economic boom here in Ireland and especially Dublin which gave way to a lot of eastern European Workers filling many jobs as there were so many to fill in my industry which was steel erecting, Anyhow during these years I got very friendly to two good guys called Rado and Brian from Slovakia As the years passed working side by side we taught each other all the bad slang words in our own languages!! Anyway to get to the point I was invited over to Slovakia numerous times as I was told it was beautiful, they had great outdoors which I was told they had wolves, bear large deer etc., I love to hike and do a little Hunting as I do here during pheasant season, so I travelled over with Rado in June 2006 for his sister's wedding I arrived at the town they lived in about 150 miles west of the airport, and realized it was more of a village rather Than a town, which disappointed me in the woman dept., lowering my chances to meet one, if you understand me?

On the other hand the scenery was stunning, heavily forested mountainous lakes etc.
We met his family and hit the nearest pub for a catch up with Rado, s friends; I could not understand a word All night but enjoyed the wheat beer, waking the next morning I decided to get up

and go for a stroll through the village, Rado, s family
and himself were all still asleep as it was about 7am
I always was an early riser, at the
End of the village there was a small trail that let off
into the forest, so I decided to walk in a little to see
what birds I could spot if any, but I could hear the
forest was waking also as the morning sounds were
refreshing to hear.

I had walked about 15 minutes or so on this small
dirt track that wound through the uphill steep climb,
when I realized how quiet it was compared to when
I had first started, no birds, insects, nothing, I
started to worry in case I got lost so Quickly spun
around and started to make my way back, when I
noticed something bipedal was walking in unison
with me, but inside the thick tree line, I stopped and
it would stop! I yelled a few choice words the guys
taught me in Slovak and carried on, every step was
copied nearly stride for stride, I stopped again and it
stopped again, at this time the tree line was kind of
thinner and I could make out a BIG black outline, 7ft
or so but in the brush so no features, I didn't need
any more hanging around and took off like a
scalded cat, I could hear my heart beat in my chest
and To my horror this thing was running also, I
could see the downhill exit out onto the cobbled
road that led into the
Village about 200 meters away, when I noticed the
heavy footfall had stopped, I looked around while
still running And to this day I wish I had not what I
saw was only side view as it was turning away back
into the thick forest, I Can still see it in my mind
today and I have goose pimples on my arms telling
it again, ok what I saw was approx.
75ft away and turning away from me, I would say it

was 7 ft. but could of been bigger or smaller as I was looking up at it, it was like a huge weightlifter from the side, huge physique, hair but not really thick and head like a fox but more slender if you can understand that, I only saw it for a second or two, when I did I actually started to cry while I ran onto the road, it made no sound whatsoever, but I do remember its muzzle, which bit like a dog, but thinner and shorter like a fox, It totally turned my world upside down I don't know what is real or not anymore, I won't even hike over here in Ireland anymore, It ruined my favorite pastime, I never mentioned it to anyone in Rado,s house, looking back I think maybe I should have, maybe they could have shed some light on the subject, but Its burned in my memory.

18 ARKANSAS BIGFOOT

We lived in the country not far from Ozark, Arkansas. Our address was Cecil, Arkansas, wherever that is. My dad worked in the oil patch and was gone at night and home during the day. It was in the summertime, and we had lived in the house for about a month. Our house was about a mile from a blacktop road, and we were the first house on the dirt road. The man who owned the house was Clyde S and he lived about a quarter mile further down the road from us, and beyond that, I don't know what other houses were on the road, but there was almost no traffic on it. There was a big field between his house and ours, and we could see his place clearly from our house. His mother lived in a little house directly across the road from him. Our house faced the north and behind us was limitless forest, pastures and ponds for miles. There was a small guest house directly behind ours that had never been finished, and beyond that was a fence with an archway over the gate. The distance from the back of our house to the fence was approximately 20 feet. About ten feet beyond the fence was where the wood line was. Along the back side of the fence there was a cow trail that led all the way down the fence to the field about fifty feet west of our house. At the edge of the field there was a barbed wire fence that ran north/south from the road back over the hill. The trail continued the entire distance up over the hill on the outside of the fence between it and the wood line. There was about six or eight feet between the barbed wire fence and the wood line going over the hill. The fence with the gate at the back of our yard was about five feet high. My mom was 5 foot 2, and her head barely topped the fence when she went through the gate.

One night, after my dad went to work, we had had supper and I was sitting out on the back porch as I always did listening to the cicadas and whip-poor-wills. It was a bright full moon. My mom and sister were doing the dishes and talking in the kitchen and the light was shining from the window out on the grass. There were always little toads hopping around at night, and I saw one in the grass by the light of the kitchen window. When I noticed it, and looked up, there was an enormous figure standing on the other side of the fence looking at me. I hadn't noticed it before, I think because it was so close to the arch over the gate that my mind didn't register it. The five-foot fence came up about to where a man's solar plexus would be, at the bottom of the chest. Add a few inches to that because the trail on the back side of the fence where he was standing was depressed a few inches lower than the fence. I would estimate that there was a good 3 feet showing above the fence at least. I had never heard about anything like this before, and I froze. We just stared at each other for 3 or 4 minutes I guess, and my sister came out the back door and told me that our mom wanted me to come in and take a bath. I said "shut up!" as quietly as I could and told her to look. When she saw it, she froze too. She was standing by a porch post and tried to hide behind it. After another couple of minutes, my mom came out and griped at me to take a bath when my sister (who was whimpering) pointed to the creature. When my mom saw him, she freaked out and grabbed both of us and dragged us into the house, locking the door.

The last look I got was the creature turning toward the field. The moon provided enough light for me to see the outline clearly. The hair blew a bit in the light breeze, and I could see it clearly on the shoulders. It was more obvious when it turned, and the hair was displaced. It was about six inches long I would guess. There was a yard light on the opposite side of the house, and when it turned, it appeared reddish instead of black. The light barely reached the back of the house, because of big trees, but it cast just enough light so I could see that glimpse of color. I didn't know what to look for then, but I remember it vividly. The head was somewhat conical, and the absence of a neck made me think of a woman with long hair flowing down her shoulders. It must have been four feet wide at the shoulders because the archway over the gate was about three feet wide, and he was half again as wide as it. I could see it blink from time to time, though I couldn't make out its face. I got a brief glimpse when it turned, and it had a flat face, but beyond that, I couldn't see. The eyes appeared to be an amber color but I could be mistaken.

I was just a kid, and I was trying to take it all in, but it was pretty shocking. I didn't sleep that night, and as soon as it was light, my sister and I crept out to see if it was still around. At the back of the fence where it had stood, there were huge tracks. We saw where it had walked away, down the cow path toward the field. I ran down to the field, and the tracks turned and disappeared into the woods. We both put our feet next to the tracks, and they were at least four times as long as mine, and very wide. They looked like giant barefoot man tracks to us. We didn't know anything about Sasquatch. I was 8 years old, but I will remember it until the day I die. When we ran back and got our mom to look at the tracks, she looked at them, and went to the barn. She brought a garden rake out and obliterated all of the tracks she could find. I never knew why, except that both my parents came from superstitious hillbilly stock, and I guess it was too much for her. She made us both swear never to tell anyone else about any of it. She told our dad that she thought someone had been messing around the house. I don't know if she ever told him the truth or not. I just wish it had happened recently, because I would have been prepared! That incident started my lifelong fascination with the big guy. It was 25 years before we talked about it, and then, only because my baby sister had never heard the story, having been born the next year, after we moved to New Mexico permanently.

I didn't get any sense that it was aggressive, or dangerous in any way. And there was no smell. The main impression I had from it then, and still do, is curiosity. Thinking about it over the years, I formed my own theory. When we had rented the house, the man said that it had been empty for ten years. I figured that it was just curious to check out the new neighbors. Now that I know more, I realized that we had heard wood knocks frequently in Arkansas. We eventually moved to New Mexico, but my grandparents would move back and forth between Oklahoma and Arkansas. I am a chronic insomniac, and always have been, and when we would visit on vacations, my nights in the summertime usually consisted of listening to the sounds of the night while everyone else slept. I heard wood knocks near Clinton, Ft. Smith and Cecil Arkansas over the years. Many times, my cousins would hear them too. Nobody knew what they were, and I never connected it to the big hairy guy. As I got older, I would prod my relatives for any little tidbits I could get out of them about strange things in the woods, and I got lucky a couple of times.

My grandmother told of an incident when my uncle was also working in the oil field and worked nights. They always lived in the country, usually in the boonies. My aunt and three cousins were home alone, and something screamed several times over the course of a couple of hours. I don't know exactly when this was, but it would've been in the 1960s. Later that night, the dog starts raising hell and there was a terrible commotion, and whatever it was, chased the dog around the house and caught it. They never found a trace of the dog, but she said my uncle found huge tracks where it had chased the dog and long, dark hair on two corners of the house where it had scraped the corner going around it. Of course nothing was done about it, and was never reported. Another instance was when someone my grandparents knew surprised one in a field at night while investigating a commotion with his cattle. It stood up right in front of him and he ran for his life, never going out after dark alone again. Both these instance occurred in Oklahoma, probably in Caddo or Grady counties.

19 THE CHETCO MONSTER

This following account is of the Chetco Monster of southwest Oregon 1890:

"The mining operation was a small one, employing a dozen men whose families lived in tents alongside the river. For several weeks nothing unusual happened. Occasionally garbage cans were overturned at night my marauding bears. Sometimes the beasts were so troublesome that an armed guard stood by while the loggers felled the big trees. At the campsite mothers watched their young children closely and forbade older boys and girls to play hide-and-seek in the forest. Even when they swam in the shallow river, an adult kept a sharp lookout for bears."

"Then one morning enormously large human footprints were discovered along the riverbanks. The loggers laughingly accused one another of having feet as big as chopping blocks. Everyone, from the oldest to the youngest in camp, measured his footprints against those of the unknown visitor. Since no one's feet were that large, one question was bandied about repeatedly: if those weren't a bear's tracks, whose were they?"

"Someone said there was a "wild" man living way up the river. He was an irritable old devil who threatened to shoot anyone who approached his cabin. No matter how bad the weather was he never wore a hat or boots. He was always bareheaded and barefooted."

"Barefooted? Then the tracks were his! With the mystery of the tracks happily solved, the people promptly forgot them. But several nights later the sound of eerie whistling and angry shrieks wakened them. In every tent men bounded out of bed and grabbed their guns, assuming there was a wounded bear nearby. No one lighted a lamp for fear of attracting the beast, and frightened children were warned not to cry. The spine-chilling noises went on and on. Sometimes they seemed close by, other times from the direction of the road or the river. But finally the sounds faded into the distance, and quiet returned to the dark campsite. "At daybreak the men gathered to talk. They debated whether it was a bear or mountain lion.

To satisfy themselves and ease their families' worries, a half dozen men searched about for bear or mountain lion tracks. They found no mountain lion spoor at all and no fresh bear tracks. However, at the edge of the clearing beyond the first stand of trees and dense undergrowth they came upon more of the giant-sized human footprints. The men debated whether it was the old recluse.

They agreed they had to catch the demented man before he killed someone. So, as quietly as possible the search party backtracked along the line of footprints. These led them out to the road several hundred yards above the camp and up the road to the logging site. Here they found where the wild man had emerged from the forest into the open area and had prowled around tree stumps, piles of bushes and the machinery used in loading the logs onto wagons.

Then the men had a nasty shock. Massive unwieldy tree limbs, far too heavy for one man to handle, had been pulled out of the tangled waste piles and either tossed aside like match sticks or used to beat on the machinery.

"The searchers followed the tracks back down the road into the forest. For the first time they noticed shrubs torn to pieces and saplings uprooted and whacked to shreds. This explained the thudding and snapping sounds heard during the night. The footprints circled the camp, went down the well-beaten path to the river turning back to the road, went down it a half mile and turned off into the forest. The men pressed on as far as they dared. However, when the tracks plunged down into a steep ravine, they stopped. The gloomy depths provided too many hiding places for a demented killer.

"The Chetco Indians believed there were man-animals in the woods, the logger informed his friends. He had heard the story from a white man whom the Indians trusted enough to take into their confidence. They claimed that for generations they had shared their hunting grounds with fierce-looking hairy creatures that walked upright like men. The strange beings were not human, nor animal, neither friendly nor hostile. They were simply there, like every other man or wild creature, so the Indians left them alone.

"But very late on the third night the frightening sounds were once again heard faintly from far off in the woods. People jerked upright in bed. As the whistling and screaming grew louder; in every tent men pulled on their trousers and boots, and readied their guns. Obviously the night howler was coming closer and closer. "When he seemed only fifty feet away, one man took desperate action. Hastily fashioning a torch of oily rags and kindling, he set fire to it. Torch in one hand and rifle in the other, he raced into the woods.

"Meantime the man's wife called for help. Within minutes several men stumbled toward her in the darkness. They groaned when they learned that their comrade had gone into the woods alone. None hesitated to follow, but minutes passed while one dashed off to fetch a lantern and others supplied themselves with extra cartridges. Finally the party headed into the forest in the direction from which the awful sounds were heard. They had covered only a short distance when the whistling and shrieking stopped.

The men halted, and listened. There was a long silence, then an outburst of bestial yowling followed by human screams. Thinking their friend was being attacked; the men fought through the undergrowth, the man with the lantern in the lead. Moments later their comrade appeared and collapsed in their arms. At first he was too terrified to speak. His companions fired their guns to drive off the howler and then waited patiently for the poor man to gasp out the details. He said that by torchlight he had followed the line of giant-sized footprints and suddenly came upon a huge creature covered with hair.

"A bear? " No, an ape! A monstrous ape, seven or eight feet tall, two axe-handles wide across the shoulders, (one axe handle measures 25 inches in length= 50 inch wide shoulders or approximate) with beady yellow eyes and bared teeth. The torchlight must have blinded it because it stood stock-still, one hand shading its eyes. Then it let out a tremendous roar. The man hurled his torch into its face, but instead of shooting at it, the frightened man ran screaming toward camp.

"While his companions did not doubt his word, they asked anxiously if he was sure the beast was an ape." Yes, he was positive. "It really looked like an ape? "Yes. An ape. "Did it have fangs?" You bet! "Claws? "The man said sarcastically that he hadn't stayed around long enough to study the brute. But after thinking it over, he said it had hands like a man, only twice as large and covered with hair right down to the fingernails.

"After that they all decided to return to camp. After much discussion the loggers agreed to take turns standing guard day and night until the ape was captured or shot. Two men would patrol the campsite on two-hour watches while the rest worked or slept. Since women present knew how to handle a gun, their assistance during the daylight hours was welcomed. The older boys and girls offered to gather firewood so that large fires could be kept blazing all night. "Nothing unusual happened during the day or the early night hours. But the two whose turn came about two A.M. asked the men they were to relieve to stand by. They wanted to slip into the woods and really search for the ape. "Reluctantly the one patrol agreed to stand by while their relief party set out on their ape hunt. The hunters carried a small lantern because without some light they could not follow any tracks. But they were careful to keep the light at ground level. Their rifles were loaded, and the safety catches thumbed back. Not long after, they came upon bits of charred cloth amidst a welter of huge footprints. This must be where their friend had thrown his torch at the monster.

Yes, there were his boot marks. After examining the area closely they found where the ape had turned deeper into the forest, instead of backtracking to the road. They followed gingerly step by step, over and around ferns, shrubs, outcroppings and rocks and massive tree trunks.

"What happened next could only be guessed. Apparently the apelike creature loomed before them. One man started shooting while the other put down the lantern and shot, too. "The patrol on guard at the campsite heard the volley of shots. They pounded each other happily. The hunters had killed the beast! But then they listened in mounting horror to frantic cries for help, which were drowned out by horrendous shrieks and roaring. The awful noises continued for some moments and then faded out. The silence was even more frightening to the guards.

They shouted for help and soon were surrounded by armed loggers and their wives. After a hasty explanation, all the men plunged into the woods, leaving the women to build up the fires and protect the children. The searchers shouted, swung lanterns and fired their guns so that their friends would know help was on the way. After advancing some distance they stopped briefly and called to the men. When neither responded, they fired shots. No answering shots were heard. Once more the party advanced. Before long they came upon a gruesome sight. Their friends were dead.

Judging from bloodstains, their bodies had been slammed against tree trunks and torn to pieces. A trail of blood-smeared footprints led off into the forest. The beast obviously had been wounded but no man present was willing to track it through the dark forest. Some did volunteer to gather up the remains of their unfortunate comrades while others returned to camp for blankets, and to break the sad news.

"Within twenty-four hours the campsite was deserted. The logging operation was moved to another location.

A professional hunter with trained hounds was hired to assist hunters in tracking down the savage beast. It was never captured nor its voice ever heard again. The most people could hope for was that it had crawled into a well-hidden lair, and died."

20 CAMPGROUND DEATHS

"In 1980-1981, I was working as a security guard on a high tension tower project here in California. I met a man who was a "cat skinner" operating a bulldozer, leveling off the pads where each of these high tension towers was to be placed. I noted he had on his pickup truck, 25-30 decals from places he had been hunting and introduced myself.

During the conversation I mentioned 'bigfoot' and he told me that in the mid to late 1970's he was doing a little poaching (with forestry officials permission in a locked and gated area near Bishop, California, they had given him a key so he could go in any time he wanted). This particular time the gate was still locked (as it always was); he let himself in with his four wheel drive pickup to the area known as Four Points.

He drove over a hill and there to his surprise were Department of the Interior vehicles and Bureau of Land management men all in their "Smokey the bear" outfits (with guns) searching a campground, the hills, mountains, roads, etc. They grabbed this hunter, took his deer rifle away from him and questioned him for 7-8 hours as to what he was doing there.

The local forestry officials identified him as a trusted

friend and he was let go, but told to "Never come back", He had determined during his interrogation that the reason the BLM and Dept. of Interior were there in force was that a Bigfoot creature had gone through there the day before and had turned over a "large" trash container (of the type you find behind large department stores - dumpsters), that no man can even begin to move and had killed several people.

Over the years the story was passed through several people, in fact "quite a few" bigfoot researchers, but "no one" was able to come up with one single "clue".

Then in early to middle 1991, a young student also interested in investigating the Bigfoot mystery, called the C.F.B.O.'s hotline to tell me that he had heard that story several years ago and it had "always" stuck with him. He went on to relate that when he was doing some bigfoot research in the town of Bishop, California (Inyo County), area in 1989-90 he met a former policeman who said he was on the Bishop police force in the mid to late 1970's. The student related the foregoing story of Bigfoot to the ex-police officer from Bishop, and he confirmed it. The officer said the story was the talk of the law enforcement agencies in that area at the time, but they were under very tight orders not to say anything about the incident and the related deaths.

Richard Grumley

1935-2000

21 THE APEMAN OF WHITEFACE

Is the "creature" a fabrication, a product of a vivid imagination, expert craftsmanship and a showman's flair for illusion? Or is it really a flesh-and-blood clue to the development of the family of man?

WANTED: DEAD OR ALIVE! The abominable snowman also known as Yeti, Oh-mah, Almasti, Sasquatch and other aliases. The fugitive is a two-footed mammal known scientifically as Homo pongoides, or "ape-like man." Suspect has been identified as a missing link between the ape and modern man. Eyewitnesses have reported that he closely resembles the Neanderthal species of sub-human.

Suspect is described as follows: Height: six to nine feet. Weight: 250 to 800 pounds. Complexion: wind-burned and ruddy. Dress: Suspect's body is covered with one-inch long reddish-brown hair except for portions of the face, hands and feet, He has been seen in the Himalayan Mountains, in Russia, the United States, and Canada.

If some persistent hunter should capture such a creature, we might expect that fame; fortune and a footnote in scientific history would be his reward. The enigma of the "missing link" has plagued scientists of the Darwinian theory for many years.

The actual body of an ape-man specimen would end this controversy and prove the existence of the abominable snowman. The rewards should be considerable.

Through pure chance and random circumstance, I obtained the body of such a creature. Two world-renowned scientists examined the corpse and declared it was a genuine ape-man creature, scientifically identified as Homo pongoides.

Belgian scientist Bernard Heuvelmans declared: "For the first time in history, a fresh corpse of a Neanderthal-like man has been found. It means that this form of Hominid, thought to be extinct since prehistoric times, is still living today. The long search for rumored 'ape-men' or 'missing links' has been successful."

Heuvelmans' associate, author and scientist Ivan Sanderson, reported in a national magazine that the creature was "the genuine article. This was no phony Chinese trick, or 'art' work."

When the newspapers published articles on my specimen, I was astonished, and then concerned, to discover the creature was labeled a "hoax"' by the prestigious Smithsonian Institution in Washington, D.C. To my knowledge no member of the Smithsonian scientific staff has ever examined the specimen described by Dr. Heuvelmans and Ivan Sanderson.

I became extremely nervous when the newspapers in both the U.S. and England pointed out that "... if this creature is real, then there may be the question of how and why it was killed." My fears led me to an attorney and personal friend who explained the possibility of a murder charge. The Federal Bureau of Investigation and hordes of lesser law enforcement officials revealed a sudden, ominous interest in my specimen, on one occasion I had to ask my U.S. Senator for his help to get me out of an untenable situation with the Bureau of Customs and The Department of Health, Education, and Welfare.

My dreams of recognition from the scientific community have vanished. My attorney adequately summed up the situation one morning: "Frank, if you're not careful you'll end up in a prison cell."

Now, for the first time I want the full story on this creature to be published. I have not asked for, and will not receive, a single cent from SAGA magazine. My main desire is to eliminate much of the supposition and conjecture about a story that has become the biggest controversy in the scientific world in the past decade.

Let us start at the beginning. In 1960, I was an Air Force Captain and pilot assigned to the 343rd

Fighter Group in Duluth, Minn. I had five years to go until my retirement as a 20-year Air Force career officer and was looking forward to a quiet life on a small farm somewhere in southern Minnesota. I enjoyed being stationed in Duluth as the hunting and fishing in northern Minnesota is the best in the world. During the 1960 deer-hunting season I was staying in a small resort on the shores of the Whiteface Reservoir, approximately 60 miles north of Duluth. Lts. Roy Aafedt and Dave Allison, and Maj. Lou Szrot were the other members of the hunting party.

We left the cabin a few minutes after six on the second morning and, although I had not spotted a deer on the opening day. I was confident that a narrow neck of swamp where I had hunted was one of the best locations in the area. I sat motionless on a hillside overlooking this pine-crested thicket for almost two hours. I was about to leave for another location when a movement at the edge of the swamp caught my eye. My pulse quickened as I thumbed for the safety catch on my customized 8mm Mauser. A large doe, partially obscured by a cedar tree, was staring directly at me.

Suddenly, a shot echoed from the other side of the swamp. With one frightened leap, the doe dashed out of the thicket and headed straight toward me; I raised my gun into firing position just as she spotted me. Making three great leaps broadside, she scrambled back toward the swamp. I fired just as she reached the edge of the trees and she fell, headlong, onto the ground. I bolted my rifle end tried to get off another shot but she was up and out of sight into the heavy brush before I could take aim.

I walked toward the thicket where I located large spots of blood on the frozen grass. I also discovered that the wounded doe had left a clear trail that led straight into the swamp. There was no snow on the ground and my borrowed compare proved useless. It was against my better judgment but I decided to follow the trail for a short distance into the swamp.

I pushed slowly along following the doe's bloody trail, expecting her to be lying just beyond the next bush. After an hour, however, I realized that it would be impossible to pack the deer out even if I did find her. I checked my bearings and decided to take just a few more steps before retracing my trail out of the Stepping over a small cedar log I heard a strange gurgling sound just ahead. Startled, I raised my gun and listened to the noise for a moment concluding that the deer went down and strangled in her own blood. Cautiously, I eased my way toward the sound.

Suddenly, I froze in horror!

In the middle of a small clearing were three hairy creatures that at first looked like bears. Two of these creatures were on their knees, tearing at the insides of a freshly killed deer. The deer's innards were scattered around the clearing and the "things" were scooping blood from the stomach cavity into the palms of their human-like hands. Raising their cupped hands of fresh blood to their mouths, they swallowed the liquid.

Without warning the male leaped straight into the air from its crouched position. His arms jerked upward, high over his head, and he let out a weird screeching sound. Screeching and screaming, he charged toward me. I cannot remember aiming my rifle nor do I recall pulling the trigger, but a bullet must have slammed into the beast's body.

As blood spurted from his face the huge creature staggered, seemingly stunned by this unexpected happening. I do not recall ejecting my spent shell nor do I recall firing my rifle again. In many sweat-drenched nightmares, however, I have vividly envisioned the blood- covered face lying on the ground beside the mutilated deer. I have absolutely no recollection of ever seeing the other two creatures again. They seemed to have vanished into "thin air."

Blind with fear, I started to run. I dashed over the swampy terrain not knowing or caring in which direction I ran. My only thought was to get away from those horrible "things." I stumbled, fell, picked myself up, and fell again. I thought they were right behind me. Finally, I fell onto the frozen marshland completely exhausted, not caring if the creatures caught me. I lay there waiting for the attack.

I have no recollection of time and perhaps my mind blanked out, when I regained composure there was only the natural silence of the swampland. I wondered if I hadn't fallen asleep and dreamed the whole thing. Regardless. I knew I must find my way out of the swamp. My compass, which I had borrowed from Major Szrot, was next to worthless. I raised my rifle and fired the three rapid shots that signal a hunter is in trouble. Nothing happened. I reloaded my rifle and fired again. This time returning shots echoed in the distance.

I moved in the direction of the shots but stopped periodically and listened intently for some familiar sound. After traveling a considerable distance. I finally heard someone calling to me. Traveling in the direction of the voice I finally emerged onto a hilly clearing and saw a group of hunters standing around their camp. I approached and, hiding my fright, explained that I had become lost from my hunting party that morning. Two of the hunters seemed to know where our green pickup was parked and volunteered to drive me back in their automobile.

It was past noon when we arrived back at our parked truck. Lou and the boys were waiting. I threw the compass at Lou. "That compass isn't worth a cent." I complained. "You're just the great white hunter who got lost." someone chuckled, chiding me for my lack of wood lore.

On several occasions that day, I started to mention my harrowing experience to my companions. I wanted to confide in someone, but how could I? Military retirement was less than five years away. I might lose everything if the story got out. The night surgeon might even believe I was mentally unstable and unfit for flying duty. I could be forced out of the Air Force on a medical discharge.

My mind reeled with the possibilities. If I returned to the swamp what would it prove? Had I killed the creature? Was it an escaped gorilla? Or was it a man dressed up for-some deer- hunting prank. Except for being completely hair-covered, the "thing" seemed to have every feature of a human being. What about the two creatures that had disappeared? Or, had the whole thing been the product of my imagination? Everything was unreal and totally incomprehensible.

Our hunting party returned home and I spent a month wrestling with my conscience. I had been troubled with migraine headaches several years previously and now they returned with a pounding intensity. I swallowed dozens of pills each day. As both an instructor and instrument check pilot I always flew as aircraft commander. I often had a pilot who was neither current, nor checked out for the particular aircraft we were flying, so I avoided airtime, except for a single four-hour flight near the end of the month.

I knew it was impossible to continue to fly until the mystery of my experience in the swamp had been resolved. I watched the weather closely, waiting for a heavy snow, which would provide good tracking conditions. I would not consider going into that swamp again without being able to backtrack in my own footsteps. On the 29th of November it happened. The weather reported five inches of fresh snow in the Whiteface area.

On Friday, December 2nd. A warm front moved in and the snow was slowly melting making ideal tracking conditions. By now I had formed a plan. The following day I took my automatic shotgun. Several rounds of double-O buckshot, hooked my swamp-buggy to the back of my pickup and with Mike, my faithful dog, headed north to Whiteface Reservoir. Passing Ranta's resort, I proceeded to the east side of the lake. After the bug was unhooked and the chains installed on the huge DC-3 aircraft tires. I headed down the old logging trail looking for the area where we had parked our truck during the hunting season.

Mike was trembling with anticipation and I was shaking with fear. Any mishap could be disastrous. It seemed doubtful that any other human would enter this portion of the woods for the rest of the winter. I was also aware of the possibility of encountering one or more of the "things" and not knowing what to expect created a fear that almost caused me to turn back.

The bug ran beautifully as I inched through the soft snow, so I turned my attention to searching for a familiar landmark. After making several lucky guesses at "Y's" in the trail I suddenly recognized the small clearing where the truck had been parked. Again, almost uncontrollable fear gripped me as I parked the bug. My heart raced wildly as I pulled my shotgun from the rack and heeded for my old stand overlooking the swamp. The old trail that had been taken by the wounded doe was covered with snow so I inched in a general direction toward the scene. It was difficult to walk, as small logs covered with snow acted as built-in obstacles. I was constantly on the alert for tracks in the melting snow. Once I fell across a snow-covered log and remained there to rest for a few minutes. Mike, working in his usual circle, jumped a browsing deer that came crashing through the thicket. My heart leaped into my throat.

The bug ran beautifully as I inched through the soft snow, so I turned my attention to searching for a familiar landmark. After making several lucky guesses at "Y's" in the trail I suddenly recognized the small clearing where the truck had been parked. Again, almost uncontrollable fear gripped me as I parked the bug. My heart raced wildly as I pulled my shotgun from the rack and heeded for my old stand overlooking the swamp. The old trail that had been taken by the wounded doe was covered with snow so I inched in a general direction toward the scene. It was difficult to walk, as small logs covered with snow acted as built-in obstacles. I was constantly on the alert for tracks in the melting snow. Once I fell across a snow-covered log and remained there to rest for a few minutes. Mike, working in his usual circle, jumped a browsing deer that came crashing through the thicket. My heart leaped into my throat.

I was ready to run when Mike started to dig at the body under the snow. I realized then that the events of that horrible day a month earlier had been real. I staggered to my feet, called Mike to my side and spent several minutes staring at the huge, hairy body. Finally I brushed the snow away from the head and noticed that one eye seemed to be completely missing. But there was so much frozen blood it was impossible to tell for sure.

The face was not covered with hair, but the neck, shoulders and stomach, were caked with frozen blood. The creature's left arm was twisted under the body but I compared the right hand with my own. This hand appeared identical to mine, except it was twice as large.

As I was inspecting the creature my fear suddenly vanished. I was now convinced I had not killed a true human being, but something similar to man, perhaps some "freak" of nature. Maybe it was a mutant of some type. I examined the poor creature and realized it was in a perfect state of preservation. I also noticed that the dead deer had been completely devoured by predators. Why hadn't these predatory animals eaten the flesh of the "hairy thing"? There was indeed a mystery surrounding this "freak."

I decided that the creature should not be left in the swamp. I was still concerned with the scandal that could jeopardize my retirement from the Air Force. It was impossible to dig a grave in the frozen earth. If the creature was left in the swamp, a wandering hunter might stumble over the body in the spring. An investigation by law officers might lead the authorities to me.

There was only one thing to do. I left the swamp buggy concealed in the woods and went back to Duluth with my pickup. I told my wife that the bug had become stuck, and I had to have a pick, shovel, ax, and chain saw. I returned to the swamp the following day and inched the bug back into the brush cutting a trail as I went. Using an ice chisel from the truck, I chopped the creature's body from the frozen earth. Loading that hulk onto the rear platform of my swamp buggy was one of the most difficult experiences of my life. The body was rough dead weight, and was frozen solid. Finally the icy form was laid out on the platform and I snugged it down with cargo straps that were standard equipment in the bug. When I reached the pickup I struggled to transfer the monstrous form to the truck bed. Again the nylon straps were indispensable.

It was after dark when I pulled up to my home in the suburban military housing area of Duluth. My wife, Irene, war almost hysterical when she saw the gigantic corpse. I was now beginning to accept the creature and finally, I convinced her of the seriousness of my experience.

"What do you plan to do with the thing?" she asked, fearfully staring at the ape-like form. "I can't dig a grave, the ground is frozen solid," I explained "Maybe we can keep it in the freezer until spring?" We had just purchased a large food freezer two weeks earlier. "But the freezer is full of meat." Irene protested. "Then we'll have to give the meat away," I answered. "My retirement is more important than a few dollars' worth of meat."

She finally agreed to my plan. Like many military wives she was accustomed to adjusting to unforeseen and unpredictable circumstances. We put our three children to bed, waited until they were asleep, and then with the use of the straps dragged the carcass of the creature into the basement.

"We'd better keep the thing covered." Irene said, as she went upstairs for an old Army blanket, "I'll keep the kids out of basement and clean out the freezer."

When I returned home after duty on Monday, I discovered my wife had cleaned out the freezer as she had promised. However, she was almost hysterical over the thought of having that horrible "thing" in the basement. "I don't know what it is," she confided, "but it smells terrible and the odor is all over the house."

Despite the stench, we entered the basement and bent the creature's arms and legs so that it would fit into the freezer. Either the body was still frozen or rigor mortis had set in. It was an extremely difficult task and we both breathed easier when the creature was completely in and the top securely fastened. We washed our hands several times and placed our clothes in the washer to soak. Later that night we opened the basement windows for a thorough airing. "Let's not tell a single person about this," I cautioned my wife. "We'll just leave it there until spring."

The creature remained in our food freezer for almost a month. Then my curiosity drew me into the basement. Man or animal? A mutant human or a cross between the ape and man family? There were a hundred different explanations. I opened the freezer and discovered the creature's body was dehydrating. Certain parts of the body looked likes piece of dried-up meat.

I went back upstairs and told Irene of the dilemma. "If we bury it in the spring it won't make any difference," I said. "But if we learn what it is and decide to keep it then it should be properly preserved. I don't know how to keep it from drying out."

My wife thought a moment. "Remember those Canadian lake trout that we kept for two years? We froze them in ice water and they stayed fresh. Perhaps the thing could be preserved that way. It's worth a try." We started by pouring 20 gallons of ice water into the freezer each day.

The job was completed within a weekend and our incredible secret was now encased in a solid block of ice safe from prying eyes and freezer burn. To make certain that no one could open the freezer; the door was locked and I kept the only key.

When the spring thaw arrived I was faced with another dilemma. It would require several days to melt the ice around the creature's body, and, in the process the basement of our home would be filled with an odorous stench. I was also concerned about the danger of burying the "thing." A passerby might see me digging a grave and alert the police.

Transporting the body from my home to a gravesite was equally dangerous. I envisioned a traffic accident, with the smelly creature tossed out on the pavement and a police officer staring at me as I fumbled for some rational explanation. My wife was now accustomed to having the creature in the freezer so I decided to leave it in the basement and not press our luck.

In the summer of 1961, we purchased a farm near Rollingstone, Minn., in preparation for my retirement. We agreed that the family would move to the farm at that time and I would commute on weekends.

I could not risk allowing a moving company to transfer our freezer so I rented a U-Haul truck and moved all of our furniture by myself. Friends helped skid the heavy "meat packed" freezer out of the basement and into the truck. A couple of fellows asked why I didn't remove the meat first but I explained that I wanted to keep it cold inside for the long trip to the farm. "Besides I couldn't seem to locate the key in all the confusion of moving. The trip from Duluth to Rollingstone took seven hours and the top layer of ice had started to melt. Friends and relatives again assisted in unloading the furniture and skidding the heavy freezer into the basement. I breathed easier when it was safely situated in the utility room of our remote farm home. I could not get by until retirement without fear of exposure. I was concerned that a power failure might occur so I purchased a standby generator to cope with such an emergency. It was also gratifying to know that it could now be buried at any time in our "back forty" without fear of being seen.

In November 1965, I retired from the Air Force after completing 20 years of active service. I joined my family at the farm end quickly became disillusioned with the inactivity of life. I now had plenty of opportunity to read and for the first time became acquainted with the many stories and legends about the so-called "Abominable Snowman." The more articles I read the more certain I became that the "thing" in our freezer was a type of snowman. I now began to make discrete inquiries about the statute of limitations on murder and learned that there was no time limit in the state of Minnesota. Because of this, the decision was made to just sit tight with our specimen safely in the freezer for a while longer.

In December 1966, I happened to meet a veteran showman who quickly recognized my boredom with civilian life and suggested that I become a full time showman by exhibiting a rare old John Deere tractor that I had acquired and loaned to the Smithsonian Institution. It had been returned to me from Washington and I was showing it on a highly selective basis. "Take your tractor on a full-time circuit of major fairs. You won't get rich but you'll have fun and discover a whole new world out there." he raid.

Suddenly a thought dawned on me. "Would some sort of a frozen hairy creature resembling a prehistoric man make a good attraction?" The showman almost choked. "It's a great idea, but where would you ever get a specimen like that?" "Perhaps I could get one made," I said, not being able to divulge my secret.

I returned home with only one thought in mind and immediately consulted with my attorney concerning the legalities of exhibiting the creature. He listened with amusement until I drove him to my farm and opened the freezer. He stared down into the cloudy ice with horrified fascination. Later, we discussed the legal aspects.

"There's always the possibility of a murder charge if this thing is judged to be human," he informed me. "Then are also laws concerning the transportation of dead bodies. I can see all sorts of legal difficulties."

"I'm convinced the creature would make a great exhibit," I said. "Isn't there any way to do it by creating a model?" He lit another cigarette and thought a moment. "You have the original body. The authorities will be after it because this thing is the scientific find of the century; however, it might be possible to create a model as you suggested. Maintain a record of the model's construction but show the real creature instead. If the officials pressure you, it's a small matter to produce photos of the model taken during different phases of fabrication." "Better than that." I replied. "I'll even exhibit the model for the first year so that it will be accepted by carnies as a 'bogus' show."

In January 1967, I made sketches of the real creature and went to Hollywood to confer with the men who make models for the motion picture industry. I talked with Bud Westmore, the director of make-up at Universal Studios. He informed me that such a model might cost up to $20.000. Westmore didn't have the time to make the creation, but he agreed to offer his technical knowledge if I needed it. He also agreed that it would be a "challenging" endeavor. I then consulted with a staff member of the Los Angeles County Museum. He suggested that I contact Howard Ball, an independent artist who was creating life-size fiberglass elephants to be displayed at the La Brea tar pits. I later engaged Ball to sculpture the carcass and mold the body.

John Chambers, a make-up artist and academy award winner from 2Oth-Century Fox suggested that a small wax studio in Los Angeles could implant the hair according to my specifications. I approached Pete and Betty Corral. They agreed to do the work and implanted each hair individually with an open-end needle. I constantly directed this portion and their work was magnificent. They were great artists and a pleasure to deal with.

By the time the model was completed, I had another worry. There was no guarantee that any exhibit would make money on the fair circuit, yet I had spent several thousand dollars, some of it borrowed, to obtain the model. Despite my misgivings, I enlisted the aid of a friend in Pasadena and we added the finishing touches to make it look as close to the specimen in my freezer as possible. The bloody eyes, broken arm, and the blood-soaked hair was carefully duplicated to match the original.

It was now time to freeze the ice around the model and this presented a few humorous moments. I rented a cold storage room from a large Los Angeles ice company and at eight a.m. one sunny morning pulled in with my monstrous creation in the rear of my station wagon. A stunned executive happened to stroll by and did several double takes. "W-w-w-w- where are you going with that thing?" he stammered. "I've rented a storage room for a few days," I explained.

"In our company?" he stared at the model and twisted his hands in anguish. "My gosh! Was that a living 'thing'? This is a food processing plant. Get that thing out of here before a government inspector sees it."

Later, I arranged to "ice down" the model at a privately owned locker plant that had recently shutdown. The final phases of my creation were completed there: I placed the model in a refrigerated "coffin" designed especially for the exhibit. This was done with heavy straps and a rented forklift. The coffin was transported in a special show trailer to Los Banos, Calif., arriving just in time for its debut with the West Coast Shows. On the 3rd of May 1967, the exhibit was opened to the public for the first time as a "What-is-it" type of show. "Where did it come from?" curious spectators inquired. "It is claimed to have been found by some Chinese fisherman in the Bering Straits," was my stock reply. My "cover" story had been created in advance and worked very well, so I stuck to it for the next two years.

As I continued along the fair circuit that year. I readily admitted to other showmen that this was a creation. All agreed it was a compelling attraction, but the model contained too many imperfections to fool anyone with an expert knowledge of anatomy.

Our tour continued until November 1967, when we closed at the Louisiana State Fair and returned to our farm home in Rollingstone for the winter. By March 1968, I had convinced myself that it was safe to substitute the real specimen for the coming fair season. I cut off refrigeration to melt the ice from both specimens and made the switch using my farm tractor loader and an "I" beam. I worked the creature into a position closely resembling the model by cutting the tendons in the arms and legs. I then started the difficult task of creating ice around the specimen. "This will be the greatest exhibit to hit the fair circuit," I said after the job was completed. "Even a trained scientist would be shocked to see this."

The 1968 season was one of the most remarkable in our history. Physicians, professors and college students came from everywhere to see the exhibit. All pondered on the possibilities of a true "missing link."

At the Oklahoma State Fair one prominent surgeon visited the exhibit on nine separate occasions. Each time he brought a different colleague. Even a high official of the State of Oklahoma tactfully suggested that we were not promoting our exhibit fully by showing it on the fair circuit. At the Kansas State Fair the county pathologist was so intrigued that he sent many of his associates to see the "creature."

Apparently the exhibit was brought to the attention of Ivan Sanderson and Bernard Heuvelmans by one of their colleagues. They called and asked permission to examine the creature. This was a grave mistake on my part. Both men were visibly impressed but made no mention of releasing a scientific report. However, Dr. Heuvelmans published an article on the "Homo pongoides," the "Ape-man" in a February 1969 bulletin of the Royal Institute of Natural Sciences of Belgium. "The long search for the rumored live 'ape-man' or 'missing link' has at last been successful." he reported.

Ivan Sanderson published an article in the May 1969, issue of Argosy magazine. "... Let me say, simply." he wrote, "that one look was actually enough to convince us that this was — from our point of view, at least — the 'genuine article.' This was no phony 'Chinese' trick or 'art' work. If nothing else confirmed this, the appalling stench of rotting flesh exuding from a point in the insulation of the coffin certainly did."

My problem started again with the publication of Heuvelmans' article. It seemed as if every newspaper, radio station, magazine and television station in the world wanted to verify the existence of the creature. Calls poured in each day from London, Tokyo, Berlin, Rome, and scores of American cities. The Smithsonian Institution requested permission to inspect the carcass. This request was promptly refused. Dozens of scientists asked permission to remove a core sample of the creature. Biologists wanted hair end blood samples.

Heuvelmans had stated in his article that it appeared that the creature had been shot. Newspapers began to speculate on the possibility that law enforcement authorities should investigate the manner in which I obtained the creature. "... If the body is that of a human being, there is the question of who shot him end whether any crime was committed," an article in the Detroit News reported.

With these events swarming into my life, I became a regular visitor to my attorney's office. His advice was clear-cut and direct. "Frank, you had better substitute the model for the real specimen and then take off for a long vacation." This sounded like good advice, so I made arrangements to make the transfer in a cold storage warehouse. The original specimen was put into a refrigerated van and sped to a hiding place away from the Midwest. Refreezing the model took several days and it was during this period that newspapers carried accounts of both me and the creature vanishing.

During the past few months I have been pressed for the conditions or circumstances under which I would consider giving the specimen up for scientific evaluation. Two conditions must be met before I would even consider such an action. One: A statement of complete amnesty for any possible violation of federal laws. Two: A statement of complete amnesty for any possible violation of state and local laws where the specimen was transported or exhibited during the 1968 fair season.

There will surely be skeptics that will brand this story a complete fabrication. Possibly it is, I am not under oath and, should the situation dictate, I will deny every word of it. But then no one can be completely certain unless my conditions of amnesty are met. In the meantime I will continue to exhibit a "hairy specimen" that I have publicly acknowledged to be a "fabricated illusion," and leave the final judgment to the viewers. If one should detect a rotting odor coming from a corner of the coffin, it is only your imagination. A new seal has been placed under the glass and the coffin is airtight.

22 Bobbie Reich

Bobby Reich Encounter #1

My first experience we were camping near Eagle Meadows, it is just past Strawberry, CA. This was July 12th, 1976.
 I was 12. The spot was a spot we camped in many times right next to a nice stream. We had 3 campers and me and my dog in a tent. The moon was bright that night, not sure if it was full but it must have been very close to it.
 Not sure of the time, but it would of been the early morning hours. I heard heavy footsteps coming off either the hill or coming down the road coming off the hill that passed our camping spot. You could hear the lava rock in the road crunching and the heavy footsteps, bipedal. It headed towards the creek. You could hear the river rock shift as it walked down to the water. Then it picked up a rock and hit another in rhythm   of 3 then a pause
 For about 10 seconds then again. It did this about 3 times. Then it got up, crossed the river rock shifting again then it was heading towards my tent. I was froze with fear, couldn't move and it was getting closer. The back of
 The tent where the moon shown on it you could see the shadow of the big tree the tent was placed by. The Bigfoot
 Crossed into that wall casting its shadow on the wall. I could see from about the chest down. Arms swaying, very

Noticeable hair all over. Needless to say
I screamed in terror. It did not finish going across
the wall of the tent, but shot straight out. My dad
came out with his gun and I made him check to see
that it was gone before I opened
 The tent and ran to the camper to stay the rest of
the night. We left the next day. No one believed
me, said it was probably a bear, but it wasn't. No
tracks could be found of anything.

Bobby Reich Encounter #2

approx. Aug 79 or 80 On buck hill at Pittville Rd and
Bridge Creek Camp, I was walking down a hill in
very dense young trees, black as night in there,
Luckily only about 50 yards deep. Before entering
this you have to walk through some heavy tall
manzanita. After getting about 1/2 way through the
dense trees I heard someone mumbling words like
totally disgusted talking to himself
Like the Tasmanian devil on the bugs bunny show)
 Walking across the path I had just crossed but in
the manzanita. What sounded like words were not
anything I could understand and i could not see
what was talking, but there were no other people in
my zone hunting or that would be in that spot. I
know it was a Bigfoot. I was walking from North to
South it was walking from West to East
I come to understand later was what they called
samurai chatter

Bobby Reich Encounter #3

Walking down a hill doing a drive with 2 others I walked out of a bunch of tall large trees crossed A small grove of tall manzanita that opened into a clear cut that was about 150 yards long 60 yards wide. On my left were tall trees and on my right were tall trees but only about 20 yards deep that opened into another clear cut.

I got about 1/3 the way down the clear cut hugging the trees on the left. When something growling behind me.

Not just any growl this was deep and vibrating very low pitched. I turned around to look and scanned the manzanita but saw nothing. And I moved away from the trees to the center of the clear cut. On high alert as I could feel I was being watched. I then saw my Uncle in the other clearing walking down. So I finished the walk down.

I hunt bear and know what they sound like and this was not a bear

Bobby Reich Encounter #4

I was a Jr. in high school the date was mid Aug. 1981. Archery season for deer. My Uncle, My future bro-in-law, and I had come back up to this zone to hunt 3 more days before season had closed. We had already hunted here for 2 weeks just a Couple of weeks at the start of the season. During our opening season hunt I found and old tree stand by a water hole and wanted to sit on it, but couldn't during the opening of the season as I rode up with someone and didn't have a way to get to the stand. So I decided to wait until we came up at the end of the season when I would have my ATV with me. So fast forward to the 2nd trip there. My first day on the stand was uneventful, saw deer come in, birds, squirrels, chipmunks etc... The 2nd day just before getting to my tree stand while on the ATV I brushed up against some buck brush and ran a thorn into my pinkie knuckle. I made it to the stand got up there and tried to cut it out with a knife, but ended up pushing it deep into the knuclke and could no longer move my finger so couldn't use my bow. So had to go back to camp and wait for the others to Take me to the hospital to get it surgically removed. Ended up cutting it out and my finger was in a splint. Ok 3 and last day on the tree stand. The part you have been waiting for. Let me explain the area so you can get an idea of what was Around. The tree stand was 5 feet off the road; build between 4 medium sized trees, so it was a pretty good sized platform. Right in front of the stand was the pond it was about 20 ft. wide and 30 feet long, mucky water. In front of that was a clear cut running East to West, approx. 200 yards long, then the clear cut hit a small hill and went up it I would say it was about 150 ft. The clear cut was approx. 100 yards wide. I sat in the tree stand facing West, the stand was at the right corner of The clear cut about 20 ft. from the right side the right side was thick trees about 25 yards deep beyond that is clearer cut.

On the left side were Thick trees. Behind the tree stand was a road running North to south and on the other side of the road was thick trees that went about 100 yards and then dropped off and a 45 degree angle to a lake a couple thousand feet lower.

I parked my ATV about 100 yards down the road to the left of the tree stand. I walk to the stand, but decided I had better relieve myself before getting into the stand. I walked into the woods behind the tree stand as I figured no deer would come from that direction due to the big drop off at the end of the woods. I walked about 35 yards into the woods did my business and buried it and then walked back to the stand and climbed the tree. I turned around and sat down just as the loudest, angriest, roar came from where I was just at. This was no bear, or mountain lion. I have hunted bear and know how they roar. This roar was like a lion on steroids. It vibrated my body. I was petrified and couldn't move. I eventually got enough to turn around and look. Barely looking over my shoulder, but I could not see past the trees I was sitting in,

I could only see the road. I was shaking, frozen in place, no animals were making noise anymore, and it was dead silent.

About 15 to 20 minutes went by and I was still scared to death. The it did it again, this time it was at the thick trees to my left just before it went up the hill, I could see nothing in the trees. Though I knew I was being watched I could feel it. Still dead silent in the woods. Approx. 30 minutes, (a life time) went by and I got a glimpse to my left near my ATV of something tall and black run across the

road towards the direction of the last roar. That's
how I know there was more than 1 of them. I got
no more than the glimpse in my periferal vision.
This was about 3 to 3:30 in the afternoon. I knew
could not stay in this tree forever and did not want
to be there come night fall. So I waited until about
1 hour after the last roar and got out of the tree
and ran for the ATV. I did not look into the woods
as I ran. I got on the ATV got the hell out of there.
I have never been back there and I never go alone
into the woods anymore.

Bobby Reich Encounter #5

I had just graduated high school so this was Mid-
August 1982. The setting Archery season. This
siting was about 1 mile North of where I ran into 2
of them in 1981. The setting we were on a logging
road that had been cut into the side of
The mountain. The same road that ran along the
tree stand I sat in the year before and met 2 angry
Bigfoot. We were headed south on the left side
there was about 5 to 10 feet of ground before it
dropped off at about a 45 degree angle
Down to a lake a couple thousand feet below
covered in younger and older trees and manzanita.
On the right was about a 6 foot bank then
manzanita with the occasional small tree, it was an
old burn area growing back the manzanita was
about 5 feet high. My sister and I were in the back
the truck. Bows on the cab and we were watching

for deer. I was on the driver Side watching down the hill, she was on the passenger side watching up the hill. My dad was driving the truck; I can't remember who was in front with him. As we were driving along we were coming up on some tall trees growing up next to the road and branches were hanging over on my side, so I was going to have to grab my bow and prepare to either move or up my Arm up to brush away the pine branches so they didn't swipe me. At that point on my side of the truck I was just having small trees may 15 to 20 feet high and manzanita. At about 30 yards from the tall trees, about large group of them thick Dense area, I glanced over to see if I needed to put my arm up or move out of the way. But when I started to look back down the hill my eyes caught Mr. Bigfoot dead in the eye. He was standing about 5 to 10 feet off the road on my side. He was by the tall trees, but behind a smaller one about 15 feet high. He had the top of the tree pulled to the side so he could see what was coming down the road. All I could see of it was the head and right shoulder. Part of the tree top he had pulled over to see us was covering his chin, another limb was covering the area between his head and shoulder, but

His shoulder was so wide it stuck out past the limb about a foot. I could not see the cone on the top of his head, it was like he had his head slightly tipped backwards and big eyes like he was in shock or surprised to see us there.

He was shiny black. Black eyes with no white, I could see nostrils but couldn't make out the nose, I could not see the lips or make them out, could of

been obstructed by the branch. He skin color on his face was black just like a gorilla. His fur was about 3 inches long on his shoulder, but seemed shorter around the face. If you watch the Patterson film you see that Patty had fur coming across her face under her nose and lip, this one didn't the face was just skin. It was just like how a gorilla's face is laid out. Any way we locked eye for a few seconds. And I looked backed down hill. I'm guessing
Because I was not believing what I am seeing. I quickly looked back and got a glimpse of what I thought was a baby jumping off it. The tree that it was standing behind was rocking back and forth. Right beside it a few feet away was another
Tree about the same size. So when I looked back I got a glimpse between the trees of a body, part of the upper arm, and part of the upper leg and back but it was like it was jumping to the ground off the big one. But the big one was gone and just
The tree top swaying back and forth. I was in shock of what I saw and backed up against my sister and looked straight ahead I did not want to be on my side of the truck when we passed that tree any second. I did take a quick sideways glance
When we passed it. There was about 10 feet between that tree and the tall trees. It was a narrow clear about 40 feet deep and ended in tall manzanita. There was nothing there. (Thank God). After listening to many many Bigfoot stories and watching
Shows. I have learned that Bigfoot and get down on all fours to run fast. So I have come the conclusion that what I thought was a baby bigfoot jumping off

the big one, was in fact the big one going down on all fours to get out of there. What I
Saw on all fours was black, but the back was silver just like a gorilla, the silver ran down the entire back and about 3 inches onto its side. I have to mention about 50 yards back from here as we were driving. On my sisters side looking up the
Hill I saw a spring I guess you could call it. The bank on her side was about 6 feet high and about 2 - 3 feet from the bank I saw what looked like a water hose turned on. It was water squirting up from the ground about the same size
Around as a water hose would do and about 8 inches high. The water was not running over the bank so it had to be going
Straight back into the ground. I think that Bigfoot was going there to get a drink when we surprised it. This was the last time that I have run into a Bigfoot.

Bobby Reich Encounter #6 Aug 13th 2017

I have had a brain tumor for the last 5ish years and have been unable to go camping, hiking or doing the outdoor things I loved to do. So I had planned a trip to go by myself to prove I can still do it. I had made plans for the
Last 2 months, and was going to go in July on the 41st anniversary of my first Bigfoot encounter. But due to forest fires I had to postpone until Aug. The campground where i had my first encounter is now a public campground with camping spots

And a bathroom. I thought that would be the best since there would be others around just in case something happened to me. I left on a Friday morning Aug 11th to the campground. I broke down just 15 miles from camp, my truck wouldn't start. The lady that ran the General store in town was a nurse, and I had already been up past my limit for my brain tumor. I had told her my story and what I was doing up there camping for. She took care of me until a tow truck arrived 4 hours later. The truck started right up when the truck driver tried it. I followed him to town and took care of the paperwork for his trouble.

He checked out my truck and said it should be ok to go camping if I wanted to. I left him detailed instructions of where II would be camping just in case I broke down there. And he said he would come and get me if I did. I felt safe so continued On to camp. When I got to camp there were 4 other groups of campers all at the far end of the camp ground, surrounding a big circle turn around for trucks and campers. I wanted to camp in the same spot I had my first encounter at, but it had No shade trees so i camped in the next one to it that did. The first night all I had energy to do was to unpack the tent sleeping stuff, ice chests, and bed. I had at this point been up 7 hours past my limit for the brain tumor. I crashed for a couple of hours. I finished setting up my tent stuff and then watched some movies until it was bedtime. The next

Morning was Saturday. I walked down the road and filmed my first encounter from the Bigfoots point of view, where it walked where it came from etc. My camp was approx. 60 feet from the bathroom, garbage cans, and recycle bins with a small bunch of willow, bushes between me and the bathrooms. The recycle bins were the bear proof variety, but the trash cans were not they were just

Those metal garbage cans with lids, there were 3 of them and they were against the bathroom wall. Well that night after going to bed I'm going to guess 1am to 3am Sunday morning. I woke to the sound of my dog doing a low growl, and the sound of small bipedal footsteps walking in front of the bathrooms heading towards the recycle bins. I got the dog quite, and listened.

Like I said whatever this was it was small, but bipedal. So at this point I'm thinking juvenile Sasquatch or small bear walking walking upright. It went to the recycle bins and I could hear it shaking them trying to get in. then it stopped.

   You could hear the small feet leave the gravel road onto the hard ground. Then the trash cans started, you could hear

The lid lift up, the be put back down on the trash can. At this point I knew it was a Sasquatch, as a bear couldn't do that.

After the 2nd lid got lifted, you could hear the small creature back up onto the gravel road and it grunted twice. I had set up

Lights outside my tent that were remote controlled so I lit them up. I'm guessing the little one got scolded by a bigger one

That was not on the gravel road. It lifted the 3 lid and set it back down, and I heard the little one walk back off the gravel road onto the hard ground. Then nothing for about 2 minutes. Then the quite of

the night was broke with a loud pop. And the cracking of a tree falling, and then the tree falling and hitting the ground. The pop I'm pretty sure was a hit on the trunk of the tree like a punch, then the tree snapped crackled and popped, just like when a tall tree is cut down and it is starting to
Break loose and fall. This was not a small tree that fell. And it was dead center of the other 4 groups of people.
Then nothing no more sounds the rest of the night. When I woke the next day 3 groups of people were gone and the other was packing to leave. I was sick, I tried to take down my camping stuff, but couldn't I went to the other camp and asked if they could load my truck and take down my camp. They did, and then I got worse while they were packing it. And I asked if they could call 911 for me. One of them climbed to the top of a mountain and got cell service and called 911 for me. I could not
Move to go look for the tree down or garbage cans as I was in severe pain and waiting for 911 to arrive.

23 Bob Titmus

He related this incident, which occurred about a year or two before the Patterson-Gimlin footage had been filmed. Titmus was sure his memory was starting to fail him, but this event he remembered perfectly.

He was deep in the backcountry of Bluff Creek by himself one afternoon; at the time he was certain there was a sasquatch or sasquatches very close by the evidence he was finding. He was so involved and so focused that he lost track of the time and the sun was starting to go down.

The density of the forest overcame him; he suddenly realized the day was getting too dark to find his way back to his main campsite. Titmus realized that he was going to have to stay put until morning because trying to find his way out in the darkness would be dangerous and foolish.

The nights can be quite cold and he really was not wearing enough clothing to just lie in the woods and try to sleep. So he began to dig a pit for him to sleep in. After he finished digging his bed he laid in it and started covering himself with a thick layer of leaves, branches and pine needles. After he finished the only part of him that was exposed was a small area around his face. He was quite comfortable, sufficiently warm enough and had no problem going to sleep.

Titmus guessed the time was probably about 1:00 a.m., when he was startled awake by the sound of something moving through the forest nearby and it seemed from the sounds to be heading in his direction. He could hear the sound of heavy footsteps crashing methodically through the forest brush, breaking limbs and so forth. At first he thought that it was a bear but it wasn't long before he realized it was too noisy for a bear. It came closer and closer... then it stopped.

Titmus could hear the thing breathing, not just breathing but also sniffing the air like it was trying to pick up a scent and now he realized that it had indeed picked up his scent but could not figure out where he was. With just his face exposed Titmus was very well concealed from what he came to understand had to be a sasquatch.

All of a sudden it started screaming, breaking branches and throwing rocks in his direction. Titmus held very still, very quiet. The sasquatch started moving around, pacing back and forth through the forest continuing to scream, bellow and throw debris. Titmus related that this behavior continued on until about an hour before daybreak. Then, as the sun began to rise and light trickled through the forest canopy, the creature went away and the forest fell silent again.

He pulled himself out of his make-shift bed in the ground and started to look around investigating the entire area. He walked in the direction of where the ruckus had come from and he could not believe his eyes.

It looked like a bulldozer had gone through the forest. Saplings had been pulled out of the ground, larger trees pushed over, broken or snapped in two. There were branches covered with hair samples and the ground was littered with footprints. It was no bear.

In later years, Titmus went back to Bluff Creek shortly after the Patterson footage had been filmed in October of 1967, - he saw the footprints on the sand bar the film subject had left and he was certain that this was the same sasquatch that he encountered the night he slept in the pit in the wilds of Bluff Creek.

24 CALIFORNIA VACATION

It was late August 1995. My wife and I went on what we thought would be our dream vacation. We flew into Portland, Oregon, and rented a car at the airport. Our plan was to sight see around Portland a few days before continuing with the rest of the vacation. Then we drove Hwy 99 west to Hwy 18 over to I-101 south we were going to take a few days to drive down to San Francisco.

So far everything was going perfect. We put lots of miles behind us before stopping in Crescent City, California that night. We stayed in a hotel just across the street from the marina.

We had dinner at the hotel restaurant while we talked about the day's adventures and what we were planning for tomorrow. Then we went back to the room to get some sleep before getting up early and starting on our way. I'm a truck driver by trade and I like to get started early before the morning traffic starts. We jumped in the car and south on 101.

It took only one minute and Mary was asleep but she told me to wake her if I saw something for her to look at. It wasn't too long after that when I spotted a beach with black sand so I pulled over and put the car in park and shut it off. I was going to wake Mary up and see if she wanted to take a walk on the beach. I just started to turn around when I saw something moving out the corner of my eye. I turned to see this big thing standing right in front of my car at first I thought it was a bear until our eyes met. I couldn't move or speak; we just locked eyes for what seemed to be forever. It stood about 6½ to 7 ft., dark brown matted hair, and was holding what looked to be sea weed which it used both hands to carry.

It didn't seem startled in fact I felt it was looking at me with anger in its eyes. It let go a snort and a glob of snot hit the windshield right in front of my face. It then took 3 or 4 steps and completely crossed the highway while it was still looking at me. It was then when I heard the squeal of tires and the beeping of a horn. The thing disappeared into the woods and I knew I wasn't the only one to see it that day. I was back on the road in a flash not even going to ask the other driver if he or she was ok. About a mile down the road a 4 wheel drive pulled up behind me with flashers on so I pulled over to the side thinking I was getting a ticket. But it was the other driver I walked to his jeep and we started to talk about the event, then my wife started to get out of the car and I told him not to say anything. I just told her I was asking questions about places to see along the way. I never told anyone about that day which I still lose sleep over. And I wish I got that guy's name and number because now I would like to talk about it.

25 WOLFGANG

August 1991 Stark County, East Canton OH near to US Route 30

It's hard to say where these stories come from. When I was younger I had always read about them with a grain of salt. I mean you never really take anything serious that you read about unknown phenomena, if you haven't experienced it. I think this just added to the surreal experience, in which I am about to finally indulge after all these years, whether anyone ever reads this or not.

I was not a Bigfoot enthusiast by nature. As any other person who has shared an experience likewise can tell you, that all changes the moment you are faced with one.

It was late August 1991 in a small town called East Canton in Northeast Ohio. I don't have an exact date. That never seemed very important to me at the time. I know it was during that month. I grew up in East Canton, and knew the surrounding forests quite well, from plenty of hiking time with my dad and friends.

It was not a good day. I had an outrageous argument with my girlfriend and simply had to take off for a while. I decided to take to the woods for the night. I sometimes liked to hike and camp by myself, but it wasn't my style at that time. I had just gotten a used Ford Tempo which instantly changed my life. My day of woodland hiking/camping was over, for now anyway. At that time, I would have preferred to hit the theater or something more entertaining and new to me as a fairly new driver. However, I didn't. I needed isolation to collect my thoughts. I packed up a small supply of gear to go camping for a night all by my lonesome.

I knew exactly where I was going, the spot was perfect. I had camped there before, countless times. About two miles from my parent's house was an endless setting of woods. In these woods was a series of old abandoned coal mines. Above these caves was a gorgeous surrounding of pine trees. I am not sure how they were able to root above these caves, but they made for an absolutely perfect setting.

Naturally, nothing makes a better bed than pine needles. All I really brought was a blanket to lie on, which was my first mistake. A machete for chopping fire wood and the standard nighttime armor, my trusty flashlight. I always like to travel light and sometimes, later regret it. You start to wish you would have brought a heavier blanket or sleeping bag when it gets cold.

My friends, Randy & Tony came with me to help set up camp. Which there wasn't much to it, I think they just wanted to hang out. So began the greatest quest of man, starting of the mystical fire. We made a huge clearing of the pine needles so there was no chance of a spark to set it off, and laid rocks around it. We were always really careful about this because we knew the owner of the land and he permitted us to hike or camp there anytime we felt like it.

The sun was setting fast. Randy and Tony had to leave because they had to work early in the morning. I was glad. Not that I didn't enjoy company, but I needed to be alone to ponder the things that man does wonder.

The fire was going real well. Since it was August, the nights would get very cold. So, fire good. Cold bad. At this point I was finding peace. It was a stressful day and well needed silence therapy. The wilderness can be intoxicating if you set your attention towards it, and a great way of getting away from everyday problems. Well not this night anyway.

At the time I had pop bottle glasses. I mean these suckers were thick. But I had perfect vision through them. Since then I have had Lasik (laser correction) surgery and you will read on my purpose for that very soon. So I took my pop bottle glasses, and very carefully laid them very close to my blanket. If you've ever owned glasses and cannot see very well, you will understand, this is insecurity.

A few twigs snapped around me. I'm not going to kid you, when you hear that kind of stuff when you are alone in the deep dark woods; it scares you for a minute. Ultimately, nothing I have not heard before. I then realized it was something small, a little rabbit or squirrel.

I was quite comfortable. I fell to sleep very fast. The doors of the unknown were about to be opened.

At 3AM I wake with a very startled, uneasy feeling. I know I didn't have a nightmare, but I had a much more intense feeling that I was rudely awaken. Nothing seemed outwardly different with the camp; however, the weird sense was there. I'd felt this peculiar sense before. I am not exaggerating, and I hope that other people that have had the same kind of experience can relate to this sense. It was the feeling of being watched, on an extreme level. Not your round about chill or alertness, I am talking an intense sensation. That tingly sensation that tells you that you are not alone and danger maybe near. This sensation was like a physical tingling behind my ears. It was like hypersensitivity. I guess like a Spidey-sense, if you will.

As all of you with glasses would know, I immediately rush to find them and jam them onto my face. Dead silence. There isn't a cricket chirping, a tree frog singing, or anything. Just cold, dead silence. I however pass it off as a bad dream. Mind you, at this point I still have not heard anything, or understand why I seem to have been rudely awakened.

I notice I am freezing. I am very cold and the fire is on its last red coals. I immediately lean over and start blowing on the coals to restart it. That's when it happened. I heard the most blood curdling scream/roar combination I have ever heard, to this day. It sounded unnatural. This "scream" will never be able to be documented on paper by anyone, for anybody to understand it, unless they hear it themselves. It was simply terrifying, and unnerving. The kind of sound that shoots right up your spine and seems to peak through your every nerve. The octave levels of this scream were beyond my comprehension. If I didn't have ears, I would have felt it.

Let me expand more on this heart stopping shrill. Your first animal instinct reaction is two choices. To curl up into a little ball and hope it goes away, which is what I was feeling at the moment. Or flee as fast as you can. Those who ever read this, which will be very few, that have experienced this will know exactly what I am talking about. This scream I imagine will haunt us for the rest of our lives. A quick note on the bizarre side. I also had the instinct to yell back. Don't ask me why. It was one of those feelings I had that I cannot explain. I did have to suppress myself to keep from yelling back. Maybe some kind of primordial defense mechanism? I'm going into weird territory here, but I felt a connection like that. Maybe someone else has felt the same, or else I am totally nuts? I am particularly interested in why I felt this. The fact is, it was a very surreal situation, and I didn't know how to react.

I remember my first thought, and that was "you've got to be "%^*#^&" kidding me." Because I have never heard anything like it in all my life. It sounded similar to the apes I would hear in old National Geographic documentaries, but much louder. This was Ohio though, not Africa. And it wasn't just once. This screaming continued in approximately 5-10 second intervals on both ends of my camp. On each end I heard rustling and shrill, as if they were screaming back and forth.

I was shocked once again when I see something thumping across the land. Fear took over. A large two legged something, thumped its way about twenty to thirty feet away through my camp. I say thumped because if you remember, I was sleeping on top of a series of caves, which essentially was like a floor. So I felt every step this creature made. It didn't swing its arms around like a gorilla, but had features similar, from what I could tell. However, I can guarantee it was no man.

It was a moonlit night so I could see that is was very large and hairy. The top of its head reminded me of a gorilla's. It was mostly hair covered with some exceptions much like an orangutan. The hair color looked black, but could have had other colors with it. All dark hair looks black at night, and all hair has many colors that people don't immediately see without observation.

It was a side view, so I did not see the eyes. I wish I could have. I cannot give you a valid height. I did not see the full height, because it was running on a ledge. So I couldn't see below its calves. All I could see is it was massive. I am giving you the best description I can give of what little time I had to observe the creature. He/she didn't pose for me. All I know if it was colossal in lean bulk and I was frightened. My only conclusion at this point was that the ridiculous myth of Bigfoot was real. That or I was losing my mind.

I was still hearing the yell from the rear of the camp as well. Which lead me to believe there was two or more. One thing I should mention is I did not smell the stench that so many encounters have mentioned. Perhaps because it was such a still windless night?

My only instinct from that noise was, get out. Whatever it was. It was saying, "You are not welcome here," In its own language. I heeded the warning. I obviously picked the wrong place to sleep.

My Dad always taught me not to run from wild animals because they sense the fear. I grabbed my flashlight, and left everything else sit, and fearfully walked out...very fast. When I was about twenty feet away from the camping area, the continuous screaming ended. The silence was comforting, to an extent. I no longer felt in the immediate danger that I thought I was in initially and I did not hear anything following. When I cleared the woods and hit the road, I ran. I ran the entire distance to my parent's home to what seemed like the hardest haul I ever pulled. My chest hurt from breathing so heavily.

I urgently beat on my Mom and Dad's locked door (I did not live there anymore). Mom rushed to the door. Naturally I had to catch my breath, but I eventually was able to recite what I just explained. Soon after, my Dad arrived home from work, and then I told him. This is coming from a nineteen year old kid mind you. They were good parents and listened. I am not so sure they believed me, but they agreed, something traumatic happened to me, to set me in such a disturbed mood. My dad had been Morel mushroom hunting for a few decades or more and had never seen anything like that before.

Time has passed. I guess it was time to write all this down. I wanted to write this mainly for myself. I want to remember it as clear as I can. Every detail I recited in this is exactly how I remember it. No exaggerations.

I would have through time, discarded this as a mere psychological episode. But I have not finished the story for you. The next day was equally thrilling. I knew that if I mentioned this to too many people it would be devastating. I had to tell someone what happened and who better to tell than your trusting best friends, right?

My two closest friends, once again were Randy & Tony. I explained this to them, and got the truthful expressions from them that I expected. Randy believed me to an extent, I think. But Tony took me for an idiot I think.

Since I still was not on speaking terms with my girlfriend, the three of us decided to go camping in the same spot together. I wasn't about to take the day and go back by myself to retrieve my precious bear blanket. The word "alone" was not an option at this point and time.

Why go back at all you ask? Well, it's like this. When a man is alone he is alone. When he is with his buddies, he is a god. Besides, I knew that lightning never strikes more than once in the same place. I mean come on; the chances of this same thing happening again were absurd. I was concerned but didn't feel like it would happen again.

That night, armed for battle, my friends and I headed for the woods once again. Much to my surprise, everything I left untouched. Nothing was out of the ordinary at all. No big fat footprints, no clumpy hair on tree branches, nothing. It was all still very dry from the summer. I've already begun to doubt my sanity. I am a skeptic, and generally believe nothing until I am presented with evidence.

That is why we all elected to bring a tape recorder this time. We bought brand new batteries for this really cheap Radio Shack piece of junk recorder and set it up by our camp.

Let me tell you a little bit about my friend Tony. Where I pack light, he is opposite. He was a Boy Scout (may have still been at the time, may still be now), and insisted on building his own personal living room right there in the woods. So where last night was blanket and machete tonight was cot, tents, army gear, pellet guns, hot dogs and chips.

Randy was very much like me. We were gung ho and liked testing ourselves with having less. It's not like one night is much of a survival test. I only explain this to you to maybe get a grip on our personalities a little. So you see we were not Bigfoot enthusiasts on the hunt for the big score. We were casually camping out, as we had done many times before.

In fact the previous night rarely entered my mind until God turned the lights out on us. So here we are, looking straight up into the starry sky through the pines, with full bellies from complimentary snacks from Tony's workplace. Once again a very clear and starry night.

Slowly we each dosed off, me being last as usual. I finally got comfortable with my surroundings. I convinced myself that the danger of last night, that still seemed all too familiar, was over. It is back to innocent camping.

3AM on the nose I awoke like clockwork. You ask, how could this be? I asked the same at that very moment, when I looked at my watch. How could this be? I woke once again at the same exact moment from the night before. With that dreaded feeling of unease...again.

The fire seemed to be in the exact same condition, the coals slowly fading away. I was very cold again. The silence was unbearable. I looked over and seen Randy was awake too. His eyes the size of quarters. He had a strange look of fear on his blood drained face. I asked what was wrong. He just replied "I don't know." It was a repeat of last night's show, which I did not want to sit through. I knew something had happened yet again, to startle us in this manner.

I start blowing on the fire. The scream bursts out just like the night previous. Once again I am in a surreal situation. Over and over I ask myself, how can this be? The scream echoes our wilderness surroundings with great intensity right when I am blowing on the fire, at the exact same time as the night before. I'm sure Bigfoot doesn't have the same synchronized Swiss Army watch strapped to his or her own wrist. So I am not sure why this happened on the nose again.

One point I would like to make, is on both nights, I was obviously rudely awaken by the scream, but couldn't remember it because I was coming out of sleep. That's the best I can conclude for waking up with that unease.

Randy hits the recorder.

We call for Tony. Nothing. We call once again. Finally Randy kicks his cot. Tony snaps angrily. "I'm awake, I'm awake!" We ask if he heard the shrill. He says he has been listening as well.

Needless to say I felt more comfortable with the situation this time. I knew I had survived the first night and chances of survival again are probably good. I'm not going to BS you though, I was still terrified. Maybe not to the extent that Tony and Randy were. We knew we had to go. The shrills were more prominent.

We urge Tony to get up but he replies in a cold dead fear "I can't move." I had really never seen anyone so scared. He really just could not move. He was paralyzed from fear (to this day he won't admit). We helped to motivate him.

There was no sign of a large two legged mammal this time. None of us planned on sticking around to test that theory. Randy grabbed the recorder. Once Tony managed to secure his feet in his boots we started our long trek out of the woods. When we were about twenty feet away from the camp, the horrendous shrills stopped...again. The only thing I take from this was, they just didn't want us there, and once we were apparently leaving, they cut out the scare tactics. It worked.

When we got to the trail, I wondered what would have happened had I looked behind us. What would I have seen on that trail if I would have simply turned my head back into that direction? Would I have seen that massive creature staring us down, that I had seen the night before? I have nightmares to this day about this question. I wish I would have looked back at that time, because it obviously wouldn't have been as horrifying as the unknown. I thought the dreams would stop once I moved out of state, but I still have them.

So now my friends believed me. It was a real rush because I really wasn't expecting it to happen twice in one life, much less two days. Tony and Randy both were walking very fast ahead of me and I tried to slow them down. I knew at this point the creatures were probably content with seeing us leave. Since we parked a car closer by this time, my exit was much quicker than the last night's.

The next morning we awoke earlier that we should have. I think we may be topped 2 hours sleep. The fact is, we were eager to go see the site.

Being late teens meant high expectations. The mission was, collect all the evidence we could find on site. Then turn in the cassette tape with our solid proof of Sasquatch calls and collect a million dollars from top paying anthropologists and newspapers all over the world. Of course this is ridiculous, but at that age, it seemed a possibility. In fact is seems people are quicker to believe in making money with get rich overnight schemes than the existence of Bigfoot.

We enter the woods treating it like a crime scene. The patch of pines looks just as we left it from a distance. No 3 inch deep massive foot prints, because the ground was incredibly dry. No patches of Yak type hair hanging from the trees. And no not even a huge nest where a tribe of Sasquatch decided to have a sleep over.

As we got closer we did find some very interesting details. The cooler was hanging open. It had been rummaged through. The hot dogs were untouched (does that tell you anything)? and the chips were scattered all over the ground. Not at all how we left it. Mind you there was no alcohol or drugs on our camp out, because none of us touched the stuff on excursions. We were too GI Joe for that. We were very conscience campers as far as neatness and tidiness goes. We ran a tight camp.

A nifty little piece of evidence was the bread bag. We had two brand new bags of bread and buns. None of us had any bread the night before. Neither of us had any bread with our dogs. The twisty tie still remained intact. There were no claw marks or reminisce of saliva. The bags had been simply pulled apart as if a human did it. Not a crumb left.

We had plenty of footage to rummage through. But we knew it wouldn't be a good idea to play Sasquatch yells out in the middle of the woods, for fear we would call the tribe. Hey, we were nineteen and twenty years old!

So when we got back we started the player. To our immediate disliking was our apparent lack of knowledge with audio expertise, the sound was much distorted. In attempt to capture every single noise we cranked the volume as high as it would go when recording. All this did was gather the sound of the motors of the machine running most of all.

But there was sound! It was not a complete failure! Immediately the haunting shrills were apparent. I felt the hair rise on the back of my neck, reliving these moments in my mind. We heard ourselves leaving the campsite yapping like the scared kids we were. Our Sasquatch calls were captured. Now what to do?

Another surprise hit us about two weeks later. With several attempts to go on another camping excursion, all failed. I am not sure if it's because we were all deep down still recuperating from our last Bigfoot adventure, or if we just were too laid back into our boring small town lives once again.

My mom called me at work and mentioned about a Bigfoot researcher being in town and he was on the six o clock news. She taped it on our old clunker Beta machine and I watched it when I got home.

Enter Robert Morgan, Anthropologist. Bigfoot hunter. It's just what we needed. I immediately called the news channel and requested Robert Morgan's phone number.

Soon after I was in touch with Morgan. He asked if I meet him at his office in the city of Canton. Apparently, there had been many sightings of Sasquatch in this area at this very time which is why he was there. This amazed me, I had no idea. He pointed out to me that there were in fact lots of sightings here and in PA. From that point on I heard stories all over from that area and in Columbiana County.

Morgan reviewed the tape & then had Randy and I fill out reports for him. Tony did not come. He was still pretty shaken up to even talk about it. In fact we have not discussed it until just recently.

The next step was revisiting the site. I had ultimately realized I had done all the right things to avoid a confrontation with a forest giant (Morgan's name for Bigfoot). He combed the site, and between that and our description of what happened, speculated that we had been involved in a territorial dispute with two or more young males. Us being the dispute. Apparently they liked the pine needle bedding more than we did, and the local water hole. What he said made sense.

Fourteen years later, the mystery is still there. What would have happened if I would have had the courage to stay? I don't know nor will I ever. I would be joking myself if I thought these days I would have stayed longer. When I close my eyes and imagine that night 11 years ago, the hair still stands on my back. The fear of the unknown always gets the best of me.

We had left Robert Morgan with our original sound recording. The next time I tried to call Morgan he had already left the state to do research elsewhere. I know it wasn't the best recording, but it was our only evidence of this encounter, and clear enough to hear. I was so excited when I heard the Columbiana County recordings because the sounds were so like ours. I recently got back in contact with Robert, and it was nice to hear he did remember us and our recordings. Morgan was extraordinarily helpful then, and even more so now.

That day was a special day for me. It showed me scientists aren't the big dogs they make themselves out to be. If there was no mystery in life then it would be too predictable for everybody. It was a day that took a large chunk out of my ordinary life and threw me right into my own X-FILE. It was scary, exciting, mysterious, thrilling and suspenseful all rolled up into one.

The skeptic in me sometimes says, I just imagined all this. It all seemed so real, but couldn't have been. The rational side of me butts in and says, this really happened, no matter how unbelievable the situation was, and my friends were there to witness it. It was amazing, and I would invite it to happen anytime of day or night again. I love the mystery of it, and that there are so many opinions out there, but I know the real truth. It's not a mystery to me at all anymore. Keeping themselves hidden so well that it lights a little flare of rich thought in all of us. These woods people have stayed hidden for as long as they need to be. They have to be really good at it to avoid all the people fighting to get footage with tripwire cameras and such.

No closing comments here. Just a great experience into the unknown, that I can call my own. That's enough for me.

26 JEVNING RESEARCH

Hutchins Sighting
2:00-2:30pm July, 2014
Route 30 South Paul Smith's NY

Nearest body of Water: Water all over the place. Road runs right through the Adirondack Park.

Would have been about 10 miles north of Saranac Lake and about 18 miles north of the Lake Placid Ski Jump.

Witness Profile: Tommy Hutchins. 36 Years old. Fishing guide from Malone. Avid outdoorsman. Hunter, Fisherman. If it's an outdoor activity he's done it. Was a complete skeptic before the incident.

Activities of witness leading to the sighting: Towing a Trailer up to go fishing for a few days by himself before his next clients came. Just rounding a large bend that wraps around a massive rock formation. Both sides of the road are thick with wild State wetlands.

On Monday of the week the sighting took place Mr. Hutchins got a phone call from a client with an emergence cancelling a trip from Tuesday to Friday morning. So he figured he may as well take advantage of the opportunity and take those days to do a little personal fishing. He hooked up the boat and headed out. He was headed to Saranac

Lake to put the boat in on the Raquet River and take the boat up through the canals that go from the first of the Saranac Lakes to the Third. As he was travelling through Paul Smith's past Paul Smiths College he was just noticing how nice of a day it was and how nice it was with no one else on the Water for a couple of days. There's this big bend in the road heading south on NY State route thirty right past the Brighton Store in Brighton NY. The bend goes around a big outcropping of rock that rests on the side of a big hill covered in spruce. Now, on to either side of the hill is nothing but gorgeous protected NYS wetlands. There's a ton of them in the Adirondack Park but this area especially. Once he got half way around the bend and it started to straighten out a bit he said he noticed something large in the tree line about 70 yards in front and to the right. It was then he said a bad feeling filled him he slammed on his breaks (which he thought was weird because it hadn't come right out yet) but he said he felt weird. He said that's when it walked out. Extremely massive immense bi pedal "creature" that was covered in a Blonde brown hair. The whole coat was not matted but he could definitely see large matter clumps all over the coat. He said the speed of the walk was weird. It was walk speed but the thing was moving its upper body like it was jogging. He said it was across the road in 2.5-3 strides. As it got to the other side that's when it got intense for him. It turned quick and looked at him before leaping 20 ft. out 20ft down off the ledge that he took right into the wetlands. He said he here the splash the books the cracks and crunches. Tommy pulls his truck of to where the creature jumped. Just as looked out about 100 meters you could see him still tearing through the last of that mud sand and water before running back into the Bush. Like Mr. Hutchins told me, He was raised just like any other Adirondack by. We were killing deer, bear, we trapping running hounds stuff like that at a very young age. On top of that he's a guide. He knows the wildlife. Like he said though. He 2went able to give clear details about the face except for the fact that it had a slight conical head but not as large as others. Plus there was a lot of hair around head. He said what really impressed him was just the way it walked. He Sid to me "Jeremiah I don't know what it is about our anatomy that's different but they walk better on two feet than we do." so I explained the differences and he said ya it all makes sense. But he was just amazed at the athleticism and power; he had never seen anything like it. He was so freaked out that he didn't want to take the time to turn the trailer around in case there was more around. The one made him uncomfortable, after we had talked for a bit he told me as soon as, He saw it he knew he wasn't looking at a human or an animal he had seen before. So I said to him so when u where on your way home did you think about what species this mystery animal u saw is from? "APE" without a doubt APE. He was so freaked out that he didn't go fishing that day and he had to reschedule his clients. He went back and measured a branch he said the creature stood about two to four inches above. He measured that at 7.5 ft. But like he said to me, he when from a total skeptic that always carried the same ignorant views. Why haven't we found bones or a body or a leg or this or that or the other thing. He said I'm a believer, went there from a full skeptic.

Jevning Research Group
Thomas Hutchins Sighting
Paul Smiths NY
JRG founder head researcher: William Jevning
Investigator documenting case: Jeremiah Fountain

Recore Sighting
4:00-5:00 pm Sept, 2013
State Route 95 West Bombay, NY
Headed right towards Mohawk Reservation

Nearest Body of water: St. Lawrence River, this route is actually where the old native line was.

Witness Profile: 18 year old male raised by good Christian family. Raised to be an avid outdoorsman. Special needs child who according to his father hasn't lied once in his life. He has harvested big game in this part of the state since he was small.

Activities of witness leading up to sighting: the first day of muzzle loader for Whitetail is also the first day of rifle season for bear. His father let him stay home. The property is dense hardwoods with a large deer population. They each went to their own stands. His dad was supposed to meet him back at their house after dark which is about a half mile walk. Like any other inpatient teenager he was getting ready to call it quits. Just then he heard branches crashing and snapping. He noticed a large black animal moving through the thicket. Before even confirming what it was he became overwhelmed with fear, not being sure why as it got closer he noticed the silence and the smell of a zoo. Not an overwhelming smell like some describe but definitely the smell of a wild musky animal. At that point it seems to stop next to a tree and not move. He felt as though it were watching him. In his words at this point I was scared s*******. At this point it walked out of the bush in that is when he realized it wasn't a bear especially when it stood up completely. But his mind still could not process what he was seeing. It showed no interest in him at all but did look his way for a quick second. Being only 40 or 50 feet away he noticed decent detail. The creature walked out diagonally away from him. The witness described it to me as a six and a half foot to seven and a half foot Harry black bipedal creature with a hairless gray face with jet black eyes that seemed to stare through him. According to him the face he saw was more human than that of an ape. With more of a round head then what is typically described. The nose being somewhere in between innate in the human proportion wise as far as arms and legs very similar to how a human being is built much different than we hear normally but upwards of five to six hundred pounds. The only way he could describe it to me was a gigantic power lifter massive shoulders that slim down to a small waist unlike the other three types. After staring at him for a few seconds it ran off along the wood line he then sat in the tree stand another 2 hours because of the fact that he was too scared to get down until his father came looking for him

Richard Encounter Report 1
Right Before sunset
Exact date - unknown. Early November 1960
Newell Road Constable, NY

Nearest body of water:
Salmon River- Large tributary of the St. Lawrence.

Sighting would have been no further than five miles from the Canadian
Point of entry in Trout River, NY.

Witness Profile: Richard 78 year old male.
Lifelong farmer. Avid outdoorsman. Trapper, fisherman
And hunter for over 70 years. Familiar with every species
of wildlife the Adirondack area has to offer. Everything from
Chipmunks to Moose.

Witness had no real knowledge of Bigfoot except what he had heard from his father and Grandfather about a hairy upright walking Humanoid creature. Plus as Richard explained the subject of Bigfoot hadn't really reached upstate NY at any large scale yet.

Activities of witness prior and leading up to
encounter:
Richard had 10 different trap lines set up around
the area of
the encounter and had decided to drive to each
location
to check them.

On the day of his encounter of his first encounter
Richard had pulled up beside a large beaver pond to
check a line of six traps that he had left in hopes of
harvesting some beaver or maybe some Fisher. He
had about a quarter mile walk into the swamp to
where he had set up his trap line. It had snowed a
few times but had not stuck yet, which is very
common in this part of the Adirondacks during that
time of year. As he walked through the swamp
closer to his trap, Richard noticed that the woods
where extremely quiet especially for a swamp. As
he approached the first trap he noticed coming from
the east was a long line of humanoid looking tracks
that where extremely large. Larger than any man.
But the odd part about ii was that the tracks where
one after another as opposed to a man's tracks
being side by side. He tried to write them off as an
anomaly with a large black bear. Even though, he
knew in his heart that something wasn't right. He
explained to me that this alone was enough to scare
"the ever loving Jesus" right out of him. Especially
for the fact that he was armed with nothing g
except an old New English Firearms .22 revolver. So
he did not want to waste any time getting down to
business. As he turned in the other direction to
proceed toward his first trap he was startled to see

that the tracks led right to the where he had left the first trap. When he walked to the spot his stomach instantly became nauseous. I don't pretend to be a trapper. I'm a hunter, never got into trapping. I have no idea of the terminology. So I will just say it exactly how Richard said it to me that when he got to the location of the first trap it was pulled off of the anchor, the pressure pan was ripped out and the leg hold was all bent and twisted. The other weird thing was that it was tossed to the side about ten feet out of the way. As he notice his anxiety and blood pressure beginning to go through the roof he then realized the tracks led straight down the trap line. The second, third and fourth traps where exactly in the same condition as the others and tossed aside also. It was then that Richard had a feeling come over him that he had never experienced in the woods before. Against his better judgment, Richard explained that against his better judgment he decided to take a look at the rest of the trap line. Even thou he could already see that the tracks led from the fourth spot to the fifth. As Richard was kneeling down inspecting the fifth busted trap his body was literally shaken by an extremely loud Long man like yell that rose in pitch as it went on with a sort of witch like cackle at the end. He explained the vocalization as throwing his equilibrium out of whack and swore the he felt it rumble through his chest almost causing him to pass out. Within 15 seconds before he had even fully regained his senses he noticed an extremely strong "earthy smell" in the air. At this time it was starting to get dark mostly because of the tree cover. But still light enough to see very well. But given the disturbing feeling something was watching him from the wood line behind him he turned his flashlight on anyway and slowly turned around to look. It was when he had turned around he was immediately disturbed and shocked at what he saw. Not 15 ft. away stood a massive, upright creature that had features of that similar to a man but then again, was nothing like a man at all. He described the creature as very heavily built with extremely long arms that held hands with the knuckles facing straight forward. The word that Richard used to describe the creatures size was immense. Richard described the hair as being around five inches long around the whole body with the ends of the strands being slightly curled. He insists the creature was no less than nine feet tall weighing no less than 800lbs. Also stating that he wouldn't be at all surprised if it was closer to 1000 lbs. Before we continued I again asked Richard about his comparison of the creature to that of a monkey. As Richard stated, during that time period and the rural area he had seen many more pictures of monkeys than apes. Leaving a large monkey as the main comparison. Now, Richard didn't come out and say it but I could see by his body language and expressions that the face of this creature had disturbed him. He said at this time it was still more on the lighter side but was darker in the swamp due to the tree cover. Therefore stating that having the flashlight helped but was adamant that either way he would have been able to get a great look at the creature anyway. At this point Richard described the eyes, which was very peculiar. As he put the light on the eyes he said he could actually see them change from black to red. The eyes as he described where set deep back. This is where it gets a little odd. Richard said to me that the only thing he could compare the creatures huge eyes too in shape, placement and proportion to the face was an extremely large cat. I have never in my life heard this comparison. He then stated that after the encounter when he was trying to make sense of it all he thought about something else with the eyes that puzzled him even more than he already was. And this kind of put goose bumps on my arms also, being that I noticed this same thing during one of my encounters, and from one other witness. It's something I've never heard aside from that. Richard said as he looked at the eyes carefully. They only seemed to blink once during the whole 15 second face to face encounter. But Richard is adamant that when it blinked the bottom eyelid came up almost half. Way and met the top eyelid almost half way. At this point (this is to what I was referring to) Richard noticed that something in or around the upper eyelid was moving a bit. What he thought was the top eyelid closing was actually something else that he could not explain. The only way he could describe it was a built in eye shield that come down from behind the upper eyelid that came down covering the whole eye. Not blocking out the red in the eye. But just dimming it. Richard noticed that when the "eye thing" as he call it came down it seemed like it rested on sort of a ridge on the bottom part of the eye. He describes the nose as extremely wide and somewhat flat. Definitely not anything like a human nose. He then mentioned the nostrils. He swears that the nostrils where turned outward diagonally but he couldn't tell it was caused by the facial expressions it was giving. As it was looking through "soul" he noticed that it had brought up the left upper lip a little bit giving him more of a sinister look. The creature seemed to be jet black with streaks of lighter colored hair in it. He was in total awe of the size of this creature. At this point, he really got nervous. He described massive shoulders with deltoids the size of basketballs. He said what really amazed him what is the width of the shoulders and the chest he swears that shoulders was no less than five feet across. He said the traps and lattisimus dorsi area was just unreal. When Richard got to that part, he described the neck muscles and muscles on the side of the back. I knew what he meant. He described the traps as slopping down all the way from the upper head area and just curved out and slopped down. What he saw of the lower body was the hip area in the quadriceps in a little bit of the knee. He explain how the back that not slope in to make a V at the hips it slow straight down to large quadriceps legs he said there was muscle in the quadriceps that we do not even have he said he was that close and he could see he definitely noticed muscles we did not have he said the legs were unbelievable. What else impressed him was the hips how large they were and how there was seemed to be muscles even on the hip area that humans don't have and he noticed when the creature did smaller movements how the hips move different than ours. Richard insists that the arms of this creature actually went below the knees not much but they did. It was actually just a few inches of the fingers that went below the knees may be right to the hand line he said. The length was impressive to him but what really impressed him were the muscles in the arm even though they were so long. It was funny the way he described this to me he was used to seeing men that were tall with long arms that where skinny. But had never been around a big foot with arms that probably went at least 50 inches around according to him. Interesting enough he did notice something unusual about the genital area. While no genitals were exposed where are the genitals were there was hair puffed out around that area that was puffy in a tad longer than the rest of the hair on the body except for the hair on the forearms which hung a little bit lower. I have never heard of that from any witness in my entire life nor have I heard it from any of my family members down at the farnor have I ever noticed anything like that it's pretty interesting. as he decided to start talking about the body hair I was relieved because that's what I was really interested in hearing about. This next description of the hair is out of the norm but I know he's not lying. He described the body hair as 4-5 inches all the way around. But insists it was a little bit curly. He also says it seemed that it looked to him that it was shedding for a new coat. He didn't see any matted hair. But he could tell it was shedding. At this point Richard started thinking about the face again. I could tell this was starting to really get to him. Even after fifty years he's still trying to wrap his head around it. I didn't want to be the one to tell him that you can try and try but he's just going to drive himself nuts. Richard explains to me how the face of the creature looked human but at the same time didn't but at the same time it also looked like an extremely large monkey. "Young man" as Richard called me explain to me that back in those days not much was known about the Apes bought a lot was known more about the monkeys so he had seen many more pictures of monkeys. So a monkey was obviously a better comparison at this time then an ape. Richard described the massive head as being shovel shaped, but noticed that the crest of the head was pointed more backwards opposed to being pointed directly upward. He said he could tell as a man that this creature was telling him that he was the alpha male of this area and to never come back and if you do I Will kill you he said that's what his gut was telling him.

The reason Richard came to this conclusion is that towards the last few seconds of the encounter the Beast flexes muscles his whole upper body up and down up and down stairs him down also and curled is the left side of his upper lip upward and gave a growl. He said it was amazing how this creature was breathing just as hard in and justice heart out while it was flexing and it wasn't flexing that you would see a human being do. He said it was almost like it was flexing every muscle in the upper body all at one time including the muscles and its facial area that's one reason why he was so intimidated that this point he said it was amazing the way this thing is flexing its muscles. Now the next thing Richard told me he was saving for a last. And now I know why. This puzzles me more than anything has puzzled me before. Richard was very insistent on the fact that the creatures beard was actually salt and pepper with a large handlebar mustache that had the ends of it pointing straight down. This made it very difficult to see the lips he could see the top lip a little bit but he said he could not see the bottom lip whatsoever call he said about the top left was it was that it was long and wide. The only time I really saw is when the creature lifted his lip to show a little bit of intimidation. You know I was very puzzled by the handlebar mustache thing until I did a little bit of research. I found it there is actually a species of macaques that have the same handlebar mustache with a beard it's exactly what he described. These macaques have the same thing which is kind of interesting. As he stood there during the stare off wondering if he was going to get his head ripped off or not, the creature turn around and proceeded to walk into the brush showing its massive bat which impressed him the most in its mass of ass area. He says it was almost like he had cargo on its back it was so muscular it was just as wide chest to back as it was shoulder to shoulder. It just walked away there was a dead tree probably 12 inches wide the creature elbowed it just putting it into smithereens and then ripped a 3-foot spruce right out of the ground as it yelled like nothing he had heard before. At that point Richard vomited and walked out. Never speaking of it until now. He never went back.

JRG Witness Report
JRG founded and head researcher- William Jevning
Adirondack group leader- Jeremiah Fountain -, also took report
NOVEMBER 1960

Richard Sighting #2
3pm Nov 12 2015
Route 37, Fort Covington NY

Nearest Body of Water
St. Lawrence
Raquet River

This encounter took place on
Richards's family homestead
where he grew up

Going into the interview for Richards second
sighting, I realized that he in fact did see something
that day back in 1960. I could tell it bothered him
awful. I offered to take a break but he insisted we
move on. Richard explained to me how over the last
50 years the encounter he had back in 1960 had
never left his mind. And I assured him that it was
normal to feel that way. That all of us that have
seen these creatures can't get it out of our head
either and won't ever be able to either. He said he
always wondered if he would ever lay eyes on one
again. He said there was a part of him that most
certainly never wanted too, being that the feeling
he experienced last time was nothing but horror
and intimidation. On the other hand he explained
that there was a part of him that did. As in his
words he described the encounter with the creature
as terrifying and humbling. But described creature
as an awesome, impressive and massive animal.
There was no doubt in his mind he said to me that

the creature was the very pinnacle of the food chain. And that at any time it could of had him. Two weeks ago, Richard got an answer to his question. He was outside next to his wood pile putting logs into the splitter. The location of the pile and splitter is around 400 meters behind his barn but only about 30 meters from the woodland. Richard examined that it was actually a beautiful day, no wind and around 40 degrees with sunshine. He said he had been running the splitter for about a half an hour when he started to feel weird. He felt like he was being watched from the Wood line behind him. He whipped around and thought he saw something hop behind a tree but couldn't be sure. Richard then explained how the second he turned to grab another log for the splitter, a stick whipped by his head and into the wood pile. He whipped around again and nothing again. He was now convinced somebody was messing with him. He told me he was pissed off at this point. As soon as he put another piece in the splitter another stick flew three inches by his head and hit the back of the splitter. This stick though was three feet long and three inches wide. As he turned around this time He was able to see a brown upright humanoid ape creature about 6.5 ft. tall turn and run back into the brush. Richard said even though he couldn't see any detail due to the fact that it moved so fast, he thought it was a female. For one he says he noticed enlarged breasts. Secondly it was built totally different than the other one. Kind of like how a human woman and human man are but totally different. As ended the interview and shook Richards hand is sincerely thanked me for taking an interest. And said to thank everybody at JRG. That we're doing a good thing. Richard says these creatures will be in his dreams the rest of his days.

JRG Adirondack Encounter Report 4
JRG Founder & Head researcher-William Jevning
Investigator on case-Jeremiah Fountain

Upstate NY Adirondack Investigation 2
Approximately 1:00 a.m.
12-17-15

Nearest body of water:
Small stream of spring water coming off the hills

Witness:
JRG Northeast Regional Director - Jeremiah
Fountain JRGadirondacksjf

Jeremiah- This is the second night going backwards from report number 1 (night 3) The night before team member Bryana LaChance and I viewed a juvenile Sasquatch crossing a large clearing (area described in prior report) Bryana, team member Cory Rochill and myself had gone to the same area to do a night investigation. When we arrived, the area was very dark and had a very eerie feel to it. This area had brought us luck in the past. As we walked around and explored the area we immediately heard a series of whistles from different directions. Not just any whistles but extremely loud whistles, similar to what I had heard on other investigations. We knew the area fairly well but it wasn't one of our areas most used. After coming upon a large clearing (mentioned and described in report 1, except was the exact opposite side of the clearing than described on report 1) we heard another whistle that sounded like it came from around 500 meters to the west. But to me it sounded almost like whatever was doing it was almost throwing its voice, almost like a ventriloquist. It was then I instructed the other two team members to start heading in the direction of the whistle. This on my part was a very poor decision. A decision that I knew better than making. At the time though I felt that I was safe as I was armed with a .44 magnum Ruger Redhawk, and opted to keep the 12 gauge with me. We also had two way radios, so we were able to get in touch with one another in case of emergency. I took a knee behind a large pile of dead logs and started to comb the area and listen. After around twenty minutes I started to hear strange chatter like noises and movement in the dead foliage on the clearing. I slowly pulled up my night vision after turning off the infrared option and pulled it up to my eye and looked into the clearing. Now I consider myself a Bigfoot researcher with significant experience and I was awestruck at what I was looking at. Not sixty meters into the clearing where four massive ape like creatures sitting in similar positions. The one second to the left being significantly larger than the rest, being shown by an extreme size difference in its massive conical shaped head and massive shoulders. Next to the large one was another that was larger than the other two but nowhere near as large as the one previously mentioned. What was odd was that it seemed like it had something clinging to or crapped over its right shoulder and something else that appeared to be some kind of growth coming out of the left shoulder area. Just then, the large on came up to a squatting position and seemed to stare in my direction which made me very uncomfortable, actually it terrified me. But for some reason it didn't stand up completely. It was just then that the object over the right shoulder and what appeared to be a growth on the right shoulder fell onto the ground with two feet. They weren't juveniles but extremely younger almost the size of a bonobo. I couldn't believe it. They were each kind of picking up earth with their long arms and tossing it into the air. At this point I was shaking extremely hard and was out of breath. The large one then came up the rest of the way and let out an extremely loud yell almost like a man with four lungs would. Even after having prior encounters in the past I panicked and the fight or flight hit hard. But I knew better than to full out run. I then began to turn around on one knee to begin to quickly get out of the area when I was suddenly hit with an almost vibration feeling through my body, a punch to the gut and instant nausea all at the same time. As I was coming out of whatever this was, there was another one that bolted out from behind a tree on two feet at first then dropping onto all fours as it crashed into the brush. At this point I ran hard in the opposite direction of the clearing not having any idea where I was running too. I called to Corey on the radio and had him fire two shots with his pistol too guide me to he and Bryana. After finding them, before explaining I ordered them to the vehicle and had Bryana drive us out. When I thought we were far enough away I had her pull over so I could vomit. After getting home I was still a mess and it was a while before I was able to fully settle down. That was the most terrifying night I had ever experienced in my life, big footing or not. It was that night that I realized even if u are armed to the teeth, if they want to grab u they are very capable of it and people need to be extremely weary and cautious when looking for these creatures. Not like the so called experts that we all hear about, that will one day pay the ultimate price for their stupidity. Because the one behind the tree had either been there or snuck up behind it not fifteen feet away from me without me even realizing it. We all need to realize when we are out there we r in there elements and we need to understand something, these are wild animals not some magic fairy of the woods. And they need to be treated with respect and caution because no different than bears or wolves, they will defend their young and their territory if need be with no hesitation.

Adirondack Team Report
Taken by Jeremiah Fountain:
Team Leader
Northeast Regional Director

January, 2015

Approximately, 7:00 a.m.
Cicero, NY

Nearest City: Syracuse, NY

Nearest body of water: Oneida Lake

Nearest Highway: NYS Intestate 87

Weather Conditions: Clear Skies, Sunny

Witness Profile: 50 Year old Construction Worker.
Lifelong outdoorsman.
Former Golden Glove Boxing Champion. Father of
two daughters. Husband,
Good family man. Been with the same job 25 years.

Knowledge of subject before encounter: Was a total
skeptic. Saw the Patterson
Film. The same things we hear often. Although he
told of a hunting trip to
A family cabin with five other buddies. One of them
came back after watch,
White as a ghost and had urinated himself. He had
insisted a Sasquatch walked fifty yards in front of
his tree stand east to west. He said it looked at him
one time and kept waling.
But they all thought he was nuts.

As told Brian:

Starting off, Brian explained to me he was outside
enjoying the fresh air, it was a very warm day for
that time of year. Especially in that part of the

state. His house is a corner lot. It's a three way intersection of Wolf creek Road that runs in the easterly, westerly direction and South bay which runs directionally north south. Intersection Wolf Creek, making the three Intersections. He said suddenly for some reason, something told him to look to his left. When he did he said he was in awe but scared to death at the same time. Which he found interest ion because when he saw it, it did not show aggressive behavior. But something inside him clicked on and told him that he should be fearful of it. He was very adamant about that. He said it crossed out of the wood on the Wolf Creek Side of the Road. It walked across the road in three strides. The creature crossed right next to the stop sign on the South Bay side of the three way. Due to the distance he was at, which he figures was around 70 meters he could not be sure, but he believes it stood about a half of a foot over the sign which this he later did measure at 7.5 ft. This if correct would make the creature around 8ft. The description of the creature is interesting. It was completely white. He said from what facial features he could make out, to him the face resembled a white gorilla, but with facial hair. The eyes on the other hand weren't "right" they were "different," in his words. Aside from that, the only thing he did mention was a slight conical head, not an extravagant one like we hear of. He said "Jeremiah, it was not afraid of me at all." He also insists it was a male, which I have to agree that's what everything points too. He was amazed at the arms, how long but how massive. He described the build as more of the barrel shape. Not as much as the "body builder or linebacker" that we hear of a lot. But he said, undoubtedly the most impressive thing about this creature was the hips and legs. He kept saying how in his opinion, it was the most graceful thin he had ever seen. On two legs or four. One thing he made me promise id mention was that he thought that a lot of people may jump to the conclusion because it was white it was Albino .He said that those eyes were anything but. I told him that was highly unlikely and that as they get older they do tend to gray and whiten. And some are just white. But like he said, it's not a fancy encounter, but it happened. I told him that these actually are what most encounters are like. He feels very credible, granted it wasn't the best detailed but I believe he was genuine.

Jevning Research Group:
Group Leader Head Researcher: William Jevning
Upstate NY, Encounter Report
Taken By:
Team Leader, Northeast Regional Director:
Jeremiah Fountain

When I met up with Jack I started off the interview in JRG fashion, with a handshake and a smile. I could tell Jack was still reluctant to do the I interview so the first thing I asked him was why he had decided to go ahead and finally meet with me face to face and throw in the extra detail. He explained to me that when he had this sighting it was a big blow to his whole world. He believes that people need to be aware of these creatures and that hopefully the word of a decorated veteran would help add credibility to our cause. The only person Jack had ever told about this sighting before doing this interview was his wife. So I said to him "ok Jack tell me all about your Sasquatch encounter." He instantly corrected Mr. and said, "I don't think it was a Sasquatch, I think it was a Yeti." So I asked him why he referred to it as a Yeti. He told me because it was a whitish grey color and that he thought Sasquatches were black and brown and that the yetis where indeed white. That right there to me adds credibility due to the fact that it shows our witness does not know anything about our field and would gain nothing by making this up. He then proceeded to tell me that there wasn't really that much to it all. Jack said they were on their way from base to a site three hours from Malmstrom which was the missile silo site. But for the sake of the report I will call it Alpha site. He said Alpha site was in the middle of nowhere. He had just become an NCO as had the other Security Police officer that he was partnered with that night. There was Jack, his partner and two missile technicians, which for the report will be referred to as specialists. It was a clear night. They pulled into the gate and turned on all of the vehicles outside spotlights. They then pulled onto a secondary road and continued down it until they arrived at the site they needed to be at. Just as they pulled in they noticed that about fifty meters away directly in the spotlights was a tall humanoid creature with fluorescent blue eyes staring at them. Almost immediately this creature turned away from them and ran toward the fence on the back side of the property which was about eighty feet away. Jack says he remembers it taking three good strides then jumping a seven foot razor wire fence. After it jumped the fence it headed straight into the Montana wilderness. All four off the men were in absolute shock. He then explained how all four men reluctantly got out of the vehicle due to the fact that protocol stated that before fully entering onto the site, a full perimeter check needed to be done. In Jack's words, they said to hell with protocol. Even though they were armed with M16-A2 rifles and 9mm Beretta pistols, they were too freaked out by this. They were going to let the specialists do the work they needed to do then head back to Malmstrom. Once they were on the site they looked for footprints. They couldn't find any. This puzzled Jack. He remembered that even though it was the dead of winter it had gotten abnormally warm that most of the snow had melted. Although the ground was still frozen. So it wasn't conducive to tracks. He said that the creature was whitish grey with long hair. But the hair was not the same length all over the body. He noticed that around the facial area and head there was a lot of hair and appeared to be not only long but very thick with a mane that went down to the shoulders. When I asked him about the head he said it did not seem to be conical but more roundish. Given the distance this was the only part other than the large blue eyes he was able to see. He couldn't see any facial detail. He told me he didn't know why but his attention was drawn toward the lower body. The hair from the pelvic region down to the top of the feet was extremely long. The last thing Jack said to me was "Mr. Fountain, I don't know anything about these things, and I can't explain what happened that night. But I do know that this thing was just immense. It blended in with its environment very well and it was the fastest thing on two legs I've ever seen. I e never seen anything move like that.)

JRG Witness Report
Jeremiah Fountain
JRG Northeast Regional Director
10-24-16

27 1949 OREGON SIGHTING

My dad has told me this story since I was a child (I am 54). He would drive by the area on our way to my Grandma's and slow down there and I remember seeing the foundation to the cabin. If it was at night he would slow down as he was telling the story and my brothers and I would encourage him to speed up and get out of there. The woods were thick, close and creepy. I have asked my dad to elaborate on the story recently. The date is iffy, as it was so long ago.

The area is on old Highway 30 that runs by Beaver Falls, in between Rainier and Clatskanie Oregon. Back then it was the main highway. My dad said he believes it had to be before November and thinks it was in the year 1949.

He was driving home late one night and it had been raining (which is common any time of year in that area). He was driving a '34 Ford. As he came around a corner, just after Beaver Falls his headlights illuminated a creature standing off the side of the road a ways (ferns were covering the lower half of its body) with "something" in the crook of his arm on the side of its body. My dad saw what he believed was long gray hair hanging down from what the creature was carrying.

The back story on this is that there was a woman that lived in a cabin off the side of the road. She raised goats and the "kids" called her the "Goat Lady". My dad immediately felt it was her the creature was holding in the crook of its arm. That lady turned up missing and was never seen again.

Mr. Hucklebridge stated that it could have been taking her, after death, to where the creatures bury their relatives. I have had other people mention this scenario. I don't know. I have no clue if this could have been the situation. My dad feels it was a creature, either having killed her or knocked her out and was not doing a friendly gesture.

To further add to the story: Within a short time of the Goat Lady disappearing there was man "over the ridge from this sighting" who was found with his head chewed off. I understand (but am not sure) that the head and body were found in different locations...like one in the yard and one in the house. the man had a dog that would not let anyone near either the body or head. I don't know if the dog had to be euthanized to get to the man. I think some action had to be taken with the dog to be able to access the man. My dad was clear on the fact that the authorities checked and it was not the dog that had killed the man, and I believe they checked and felt it wasn't a bear either.

I asked my dad what was his first thought when he saw the creature and he said "Ford, don't fail me now!" He had fears of engine failure, flat tire, or anything else that would hamper his escape.

My dad said that he "knew" what it was, even though this was before the hoopla at Bluff Creek with the road builders and the Patterson-Gimlin film. There had been other reported sightings around the area.

He told me of a story of some high school kids swimming on Beaver Creek. One girl didn't want to swim and was sitting at a picnic table and her friends were all swimming (he even elaborated on some of their names). She looked up and a few feet away from her was a creature holding back some bushes looking at her. She let out a scream of all screams. Her friends came running up from the creek. After she screamed the creature let go of the bushes and disappeared into the dense woods. When her friends got to her she was so traumatized she couldn't tell them what happened. She was crying and terribly upset. They took her into Clatskanie and after they got to "Brock's" (Dad called it-a little soda shop that served burgers and stuff) she finally got calmed down enough to tell them what had happened.

My dad's mind is very sharp. The difficulty in remembering the dates has to do with so much time having passed. He is very literate and intelligent. My dad is a down to earth person. He hunted for many years around Saddle Mountain and the Mist area. If you know the area, it is thick rain forest. He knows what a bear looks like and knows what he saw was a Bigfoot as he calls it now.

28 FLORIDA SKUNK APE

I'm originally from Southern Illinois and became interested in Sasquatch after the whole Big Muddy Monster thing in Illinois in the early 1970s. I was about 6 when those events occurred and for a while it was big news. I remember my dad watching shows about Bigfoot (and my mother scoffing) during that time. I started reading everything I could find and that continued through my middle school years and our move to Florida when I was 11. I don't recall ever having an experience in Illinois, other than a vague impression of being watched from the woods as my brother and I played at a playground in a camping area.

Once we got to Florida, things changed. I had absolutely no clue that these creatures were here. None. Not until much later. My mother's parents had moved down a year prior to us moving and had purchased land adjacent to property owned by my grandmother's youngest brother and his family. My parents also purchased land adjacent to both properties. My uncle and my grandparent's properties had been cleared and totaled together roughly 3 or so acres. My folks bought a 4 acre plot that consisted of land that had been mined for phosphate so many years prior that the mining had been done with horse-drawn equipment and the land had been allowed to return to its wild state. There was ridge that ran about 3 or so miles from some orange groves to the west to the end of my folks' property line and behind the ridge was swamp. There was a dirt road leading in to the property which is still there and is my folks' driveway. My siblings and I, before my parents had the house built, used to roam the drier areas of this property and the property to the west of it. I recall one day being on the dirt road and hearing something just beating the hell out of a tree trunk with a branch. We got spooked having no clue what could be doing that, and we took off back to our grandparents' house and spent the rest of the afternoon indoors. I was roughly 12 or 13 at the time, my brother was 10 or 11 and my sister would have been 7 or 8. One of my brother's friends was also with us that time.

A few years later, when I was 15 or so, I found a track on the property west of my folks' place. Didn't see anything else at that time but this was after the house was built and I had heard plenty of odd noises over the couple of years I had lived out there by that time. A friend of mine and I also got chased out of the woods on that property by something big about a year or so after I found the track.

Fast forward to when I'm in my 30s, married with a small daughter, and living elsewhere in the area. My grandmother was still living at the time and had been given a computer by one of our cousins. Having no use for it, she gave it to me. I was to pick it up one evening and arrived a bit early. My grandmother and my parents were out to dinner so while I waited for them to come home, I let my daughter, who was about 2-2 1/2, play in the sandbox by my parent's front deck while I sat in the large A-frame swing a few feet away. It was early summer, so it didn't get dark until after 8pm. It was just starting to get towards dusk and you could hear insects and birds. I was just sitting there enjoying the evening and listening to my daughter chattering to her toys when the hair on the back of my neck stood up and the insects went silent. I got a really strong sense of being watched coming from the far west side of the property. We were on the east end, almost to the property line. What really struck me as weird was that my folks' dogs, two 70lb boxers, were silent as well. I started to get really nervous, mostly because my daughter was there. I didn't at that time have a key to my folks' house or I'd have been inside and getting one of my dad's rifles, which I do know well how to use. Instead, since I did have a key to my grandmother's house and since my car was parked there anyway, I told my daughter that the mosquitos were coming out and we needed to go in. I didn't want her scared, and I didn't want whatever was watching us to think I was as scared as I was because I didn't want to provoke a predatory response. We calmly put the lid on the sandbox and walked back down to my grandmother's house, with me keeping myself between my daughter and the trees. Once we were in the house, I turned the TV on for my daughter and was getting her a snack when the most god-awful scream I have ever heard in my life came from outside. It shook the glass in the windows, it was that loud. I told my daughter it was an owl, but that was no owl. About 20 minutes later, I heard the automatic door open in the garage and my dad pulled my grandmother's car in.

I didn't really want to go outside but I didn't want to deal with my mother's skepticism and sarcasm either so I went and everything was normal again. I loaded the computer and left pretty quickly.

About 6 months after that I was ghost hunting with my best friend about 20 or so miles south (this is in central Florida, south of the Green Swamp) in a cemetery adjacent to an old church. The cemetery was bordered on 3 sides by woods and there was a creek running along the rest side that I'm pretty sure runs into the Alafia River at some point. We were sitting in the car and I was watching the cemetery while my bestie was watching the tree line. I saw movement in the center of the cemetery but before I could mention it, my bestie said that a tree was moving on her side. I looked over, but it had stopped so I looked back towards the cemetery. I had been there many times, both at night and during the day, and knee the layout well. In the center, there was an evergreen bush that stood about 7 feet tall. When I looked back, there was a figure standing next to the bush, and it was about a foot taller than the bush. It was dark, so I could only see the silhouette of the figure: head directly on the shoulders, massive shoulders, long arms and covered with hair. I said something like: I'm seeing something I didn't notice before. My bestie turns to look (she was the driver) and says: Holy shit! I said: Time to leave. She started the car and we peeled out. The whole way back, we went back and forth about did we really see what we thought we saw? I went back during the day about a week later and took pictures, which I still have now 13 years later, of my daughter standing where this thing stood. She was exactly 3 feet tall at the time and would have stood mid-thigh level on this thing.

I have had no other experiences since then. My parents still live on the same property and my sister now lives on the property that my grandparents owned. There are fewer people out there now than there were, the water management agency used eminent domain to purchase all but 2 or 3 of the houses on the one street south of my folks' property because they were raising the level of the lake across the highway. There's a dump east of this area too, about a mile or two east, and a wildlife preserve. There is a series of lakes and creeks that connects this area to the Green Swamp to the north and to the Peace River to the south. The most recent sighting of a skunk ape that I know of was in 2013 and less than 2 miles as the crow flies south of there.

29 DIANE

I've had a few encounters with Sasquatch; I think that's what it was, in my life. The first one was when I was 7 or 8 years old and we were camping in The Santiam area. My Dad was a log truck driver for about 40 years and would take us deep into the woods, sometimes, to camp or picnic. I could not see and I didn't get eye glasses until I was about 11 or 12 years old. Anyway, I wandered away from the camp area one day but not too far. I could still see the blurry outline of my family. My other siblings were already gone on their day hikes and I saw and heard my 4 older brothers walk in the other direction. My sister and baby brother were with my mom and Dad at the camp area.

I was wandering around near the edge of the woods but this time there were small rocks and sticks being thrown at me. I was surprised to see them and looked at them, closely. I didn't feel safe and so went back to the main camp where my family was. I knew nothing of Sasquatch. When we packed up and were heading home in the car a few days later, I asked my mom "Can bears throw rocks"? All of my siblings roared with laughter. I felt mad and ashamed at the same time when they ALL laughed at me. I was puzzled about what had happened to me and didn't say any more about it.

They teased me about this all of my life. It wasn't until many years ago, I figured out what it was.

Then in 1988, my sister and I were taking a morning drive up to Spirit Mountain where we thought we would enjoy the quiet scenery and then turn around and go back to my mom's trailer house. I was visiting them from outta town.

I wasn't driving very fast and as we turned the car around the bottom of Spirit Mountain to drive up the road this fear overcame me. I quickly scanned the forest with my eyes and knew something was wrong. My hair stood on end and then it was slow motion atmosphere. My sister and I looked to the right of my car, like we were one unit and I asked her, "What is that"? She replied, "It's a young Sasquatch". It looked at us with a surprise look on its face. I was perplexed as I had not even thought of them before. It squatted down briefly but then quickly got up and ran away. It was reddish in color. My sister wanted away from that area and yelled at me to drive fast or something like that. I was still staring at the area where it was at, as she was screaming at me. It happened so fast!

Two of my sisters have heard the yells and screams in a place known as The Hideout but it was called that mainly due to so many bears living there. It was where my mom used to live for decades.

Then I had another experience and not sure if this was a bear or Sasquatch. It was 1999, I think. We were camping near the beach on The Oregon Coast. We drove down after work and so we got the last camping spot which wasn't ideal and it would be dusk in another hour or so. It was right next to very tall sea grass and the Jetty. The people closest to the ocean were a couple and a young boy and girl. In the middle of the night, the little girl was screaming hysterically and this woke me up. I peeked through my tent and was watching and trying to listening to them all. To my amazement they all just got into their car and drove off! They left everything! I thought "This can't be good". The little girl was still upset and crying and I felt this fear overcome me as I could hear something walk my way. My husband was with me in our tent but he snored VERY LOUD so it was hard for me to make out what I was trying to listen to. My daughter and her boyfriend were in a small tent next to ours and she also felt uneasy as she later told me. She woke-up her boyfriend, Jamie and told him something was wrong. He didn't believe her. She got his truck keys anyway from him and she slept in the truck in the front cab. She told me "I didn't care; I wasn't going to sleep in the tent the rest of that night".

This thing stunk badly and it seemed to hang

around for a little while but it eventually went away, it was getting close to daylight by then. I was ever so glad because I was lying on my side and my whole body went numb because I did not move. I was sweating and thought it could probably smell my fear and hear my heartbeat! I did pray for all of us to be safe over and over during that time. My husband didn't believe me or my daughter the next day and this pissed me off. I was confused and a little shaken still the next day.

Fast forward to current day... I live in Fairview near Fairview Lake and close to railroad tracks. The RR tracks are about 400 feet from my condo. Ever since we moved here, from day one, I've told my family that I feel like I'm being watched. It's an uneasy feeling. My brother has teased me and said "Yes there's a man out there watching you"! I replied "I didn't say it was a person. I said, I feel like I'm being watched sometimes". Early one morning, recently, it was still dark out and my son was going to work and he had to get his car outta the garage. My car was parked in the driveway. So he woke me up and I moved my car, he drives off and I had some card board boxes in my trunk that I wanted to recycle. We live on a private drive where it's only for residents of the condos here and very little traffic other than that. I popped open my trunk and I had this strange feeling and at that SAME time I hear this "Woop" sound. My back was turned to the tree line where the RR tracks are and I quickly looked back as I closed the trunk and ran into my house as my boxes slammed into my side view mirror on the car. I didn't care! I wanted in my house! I never stopped to see if there was any damage to my mirror or anything!

I've also heard tree knocks a few times. I sleep with my window open at night because I'm on the 2nd floor and it gets hot in my room.

They are real...whatever they are.

30 PENNSYLVANIA ENCOUNTERS

First Encounter

It was September 15, 1988 at approximately 8:30 in the evening.....beginning of dusk in McKean county, Pa. near Clermont, Pa. My Husband and I had ask my uncle if we could set our Bonanza 20 foot camper by his hunting camp for a few days until our spot opened up at Red Bridge, Kinzua Park, just outside of Kane, Pa. We arrived there in the late afternoon, set up the camper, and ate supper. My husband was very tired so he went to bed early. The bed was at the back of the camper where the big window was located. I always slept by the window because I can't breathe too well. But this night I left the window closed.

I sat there on the big air mattress, looking up at the mountain behind Mr. Herzog's farm, where there was a hillside to my right. I noticed some turkey vultures in a circle up on the mountain top and thought there must be a fresh kill there. It was getting a little darker but the moon cast a haze over the camper by the pasture's fence line. I was getting tired myself so I reached down to pull up the blanket to my chest, when I looked out the window I saw this huge figure, not more than six to eight feet away, standing upright and staring at me through the window. I just sat there squinting my eyes wondering what the hell this is.

My first thought was maybe someone like a peeping tom followed us here, playing a trick or something. Then when I looked to see if my husband was still sleeping, I started kicking him, trying to get him up so he could go check. When I looked back at the window the figure got closer, it was huge, and covered with long black hair, had a human like face and the moon light shined on his eyes like a flashlight would a deer when you go spotting deer.

He started to move even closer, like almost three feet from my window now, I looked him right in his face, he bent down and I could see his eyes were actually brown and his face covered with shorter hair, a flat nose and his mouth was slimmer and he had a wide face with hair growing from his forehead back from his face. It was then I realized this is no human. I still had my blanket in my left hand, and slowly I leaned back in bed with a small opening so I could still see him. I thought maybe if I scare it, it'll go away so I took the blanket threw it up at the window. When it fell down he was gone. I heard thump, thump, and gone.

When I tried to wake my husband he said, quit kicking go to sleep, now. Yes sure, after this? I stayed awake all night. Next morning I told my other half what I saw, he said oh it's just the mop hanging on the clothes line. We walked outside to see the mop and the clothes line were hanging on the outhouse. Nowhere near the camper. Mike said "How could anybody see inside the window? This camper sets four feet off the ground and you can't see in the window and your five feet tall? Nobody' is 8 feet tall, you're delusional."   I looked for

A track all over that place, but the ground was really hard from no rain.

Second Encounter

It was in the fall of 1990 that we brought our new mobile home to these two acres, I remember this one because... it wasn't just the shock of seeing this big grey human like creature with hardly any hair on him, and you could actually see how muscular his whole body was.

There was a full moon, like a Harvest Moon or something, real bright outside. It was around 12:30 or 1:30 am. I couldn't sleep; it was hot and stuffy so I opened up my bedroom window. I heard something on the roof of the trailer. It took two steps on the roof and then a loud thump. It fell off the roof or slid off it and it fell above the kitchen to the ground.

The mobile home, sat high off the ground, because of the lay of the land, especially in the back end where my beds are. I looked out the bedroom window, and there standing looking at me approximately 20 feet away from the back of the mobile home was this huge grey figure! I thought what the heck is a naked grey looking thing, that looks like a giant man doing out this late at night by our mobile home? He had to be around nine feet tall or more. No... I said, I'm going crazy; I must be dreaming or something until he started to walk toward the window. I jumped out of the bed, and shook my husband... get up I yelled, there's something out there and he's big and naked.

Get up... I urged him and I said, you better take a gun with you. Half asleep, he finally got to the kitchen door, and I opened the living room door which is at the rear of the mobile home by the bath room hall way. There I saw it, standing there bear naked, this huge, and I mean huge figure of a giant standing in the driveway with his back to me.

That thing looked at me, and when it did he turned his whole upper body around from his waist up. He took three steps and he was gone into the pines. Just gone that fast!

I then hear my husband come around the front of the mobile home, I said, "DID YOU SEE IT? DID YOU SEE IT?

He said nowhere is it? He just missed it by seconds I was so upset at my husband for not being a little quicker. Actually I think he was a little apprehensive about going out there in the half lit night looking for this creature. Later I thought... what the hell did I just see? When I told him what I saw he thought I was crazy and dreaming. He told me to go back to sleep and don't bother him anymore.

The next morning, I went out and looked where I thought the thing was on the roof. Above the kitchen window was a dent, like the shape of someone's buttocks. I showed my husband he said maybe it was a bear or something. When I told my brother and sister they said, it was a big foot. I told them that this thing was even bigger than the one I saw in McKean County. Also, this one was grey and it didn't have real long hair...plus it looked more human like, and it was really big. I mean it looked like a giant. It was nine or ten feet tall. Years later when my sister told me to go into a big foot web site... I looked up my area and seen that some campers right below us near the Clarion River had seen a big grey thing by their camp with huge legs. It was pounding on their camp.

I thought this was the last of the big foots and I could now get over it and live a half safe life. I guess I really didn't want to believe all the big foot hype, and stories and my husband said, it was only my imagination. So I dropped the whole thing. Thinking this was the end of it...but it wasn't the end of it.

Third Encounter

It was two and a half weeks before deer hunting season. All the campers and hunters would come up on the weekends to sight their rifles in. The loud noises rang out with shots being fired, then on the Monday through the following Thursday, it was peaceful again. This sighting of big foot had to be on either Monday or Thursday, more likely on Thursday but I am not exactly sure, all I know is what I saw and what happened that day in broad day light.

I was in the kitchen doing dishes, and had the front door open so the dog, a Rottweiler could see out. She loves to lay by the door watching for squirrels. I heard my one horse whinnying really loud and almost like she was frightened to death. Then she started kicking the stall really hard. Then the dog went crazy... her fur was up and she was just carrying on so badly she broke the screen door.

I went over to look out the door and OMG the smell. I will never smell anything so awful again. Talk about a dump site, an old wet dog or bear, a skunk and a dead animal all wrapped up into one, you got it. Then I thought, well why would the horse and the dog be so upset? So I went to the window in the kitchen and the dog is by the back door, digging to get out going after something. It was all I could do to keep her from bolting out the door. I didn't see anything out the window so I went out on the sun porch to have a look, I didn't see anything in the back pasture, or the field, when I started back in, I looked toward the back acre along my fence line, toward the other property owners ATV path, and deer stand.

I saw it, oh Lord I got chills up my legs and back right now, I can't shake them. Just talking about this is hard for me, because people laugh at me say I am delusional and make fun of me. I just don't like to talk about it, but I have to get this out, and let it go already. There in the woods was the big foot, big tall about eight feet or more, covered with long black hair. His right arm swinging below his waist line, almost to his knees. He took no more than five or six steps and he was gone out of my sight behind the trees.

I went down to the barn, my Misty horse was still wide eyed but she was calmed down now. The dog came with me sniffing the air and looking off toward the back acre. I came up to the house a bit shaken but now I knew that I wasn't crazy, and if I am so is all these other people. For anyone who is still a skeptic, keep being a skeptic because when they finally see one, it won't be so funny. I had one more sighting it was brief, but it was real.

Fourth Encounter

It was just last year; my husband had his eighth operation... this time a hernia. I went to pick him up at the Clarion Hospital. I was driving around 40 miles an hour because from Marienville to our home is a very winding road. You have to slow down when you come to a bend and stay over so you do not run into a logging truck, or gas drilling truck.

As we rounded the bend and started up the little grade by Buzzard Swamp, there out of the corner of my eyes, off to my right, on the berm of the road, I saw it again. Before I could alert my husband who had his head down reading, the creature had stepped off the berm and down he went. I was going too fast to stop and there wasn't any place to pull off the road. Had it been a different situation and I wasn't bringing my husband home after just being operated on, I would have stopped that car got out. Being as angry as I am, because it looks like I am a kook or a nut, I think I would have tried to follow the thing in the woods until I found tracks, just to prove to myself... that I'm not imagining this.

End Of my Big Foot Encounters, I hope.

31 MILITARY ENCOUNTER

I joined right out of high school before I had even turned 18, and wanted to get out and see the world and get out of Indiana. I did my basic training at Fort Benning (like all Infantrymen) and was stationed at Fort Drum, in New York. In 2004, my unit deployed to Iraq and we spent a year operating in and outside of Baghdad. I was wounded in April of 2005, and we returned in June of that year. By that point, I had been promoted to Specialist with a waiver, and was in a Team Leader position, due to being one of the more "squared away" guys as they say. After the deployment, our unit saw a lot of turnover (guys leaving for other units, people reenlisting to go other places) which is normal for that sort of thing. Our unit had been given the East Coast QRF (Quick Reaction Force) after the 82nd Airborne had been called to help after Katrina hit... which meant that we weren't going to be deployed again right away, and that we would be doing a lot of training on post.

In the middle of September 2005, I got called in to

my 1st Sergeant's office during a workday out of the blue. Usually, that only happens when you're in trouble. So, naturally, I was nervous. He told me that I was being assigned an additional duty assignment detail from S-1 and gave me some orders with the number to contact the 1LT in charge of the detail. He didn't really know much more about it, other than that they needed someone from the company with a Security Clearance, and since I had attended Javelin Trainers course, and wasn't a screw up, they picked me. The orders didn't really say much (I'll attach the copy I have of them at the end of this) so after I got out of the First Sergeant's office, I was just relieved to not be in trouble. I pretty much just figured I'd be pulling fireguard duty for a bunch of government contractors while they researched birds or turtles or something (a lot of that stuff had been going on at Drum anyway because of the expansion of the base). I didn't think much of it, but figured it would at least be something different to do.

I called the 1LT from the paper and talked to him about the assignment, he told me that I would be attached under his command starting the 14th and ending once the detail was completed. He was from one of the other Infantry Battalion's HHC units and asked if I could break away from my duties and come meet him in order to pick up a packing list and fill out some other paperwork. I asked my Platoon Sergeant, and he said it was fine, and since I would be assigned to the LT that following

Monday, I may as well go ahead. So I went and met up with him, and got all my paperwork filled out, and got the packing list, and found out when the next time I needed to meet with him was, which turned out to be the following morning at the Brigade HQ. Beyond that stuff, he didn't really say much of anything.

So, the next morning I meet up at the Brigade HQ, and met the rest of the guys who got picked from the different units to be a part of the detail. It was all Infantry guys, and one Medic. The LT had us all load up in a LMTV (a truck) and we head out to one of the Ranges. Which turns out to be one of the furthest Ranges on the entire installation. It's like a thirty to forty minute drive out there from main post and gets to be pretty much out in the middle of nowhere. They use those ranges for a lot of different types of training, and most of it is combat related stuff. Most of the Ranges have buildings that are used for briefings, preparations, and for when it's cold out. There were a bunch of civilian POVs and trucks outside of the building, when we got inside, they had a bunch of chairs and tables set up. A lot of people were milling about and talking amongst themselves when we came inside, and we were shuffled in seats at the back of the rows. The LT went up to the front, and spoke with a couple of people, which I assumed at the time were in charge (which turned out to be true).

I had learned (up to that point in my Army career)

that it was best just to keep your mouth shut, ears open, and do what you are told and you'll go a long way. And I figured that whatever we were doing, it would be a good chance to maybe get some special recognition, as it was apparent that whoever all these people were, they were important. I was planning on going to the promotion board soon and becoming a Sergeant, so whatever I could do to stand out, I was going to do it. That included, sitting around and listening to a bunch of scientists lecture on boring subjects or guard a bunch of tents or roads all day and night for a couple of weeks while they research stuff.

But, once the first person started to talk, I knew right away that we were listening to something completely unexpected and not normal. The first person to talk was an Agent from the 10th Mountain Criminal Investigation Command, or CID. He went over the seriousness of Security Clearances, and the sensitive nature of them and what it means to breach them. In hindsight, I may or may not be doing now, and has played a major role in what has been keeping me from telling this story for so many years. The next person to speak was a scientist or something like that from either the U.S. Fish and Wildlife Service, or Bureau of Land Management (I don't remember which) talking about the nature of what they do, and what the impact of their research means to the environment means. I don't exactly remember much, as it doesn't really matter too much to the story.

Finally, another person got up to speak; this person was a Special Agent with the U.S. Fish and Wildlife Service. They had a PowerPoint presentation (the others did as well) ready to go. They told us that in August, some Soldiers conducting rifle qualifications at a Range had witnessed what they first thought was a bear downrange and issued a cease fire (which was the standard operating procedure). They stated (all later in written form by the Company Commander) that they witnessed the animal "stand up" and proceed to "walk like a human at a steady rate" from one tree line to the other. They had made jokes with each other that they had just seen a "Big Foot" and that they should have shot it. The CO contacted Range Control and told them that they had witnessed what was at first believed to be a bear, but was unusual in size, gait, and appearance. The CO was asked by the Range Control Officer to make a written statement, which was later passed on to 10th Mountain Headquarters.

Apparently, whenever something like this is sighted, Range Control is supposed to notify the Post Commander's Office and let them know (not sure if that is an Army or Military wide thing, since this is my only experience, but if it's a Directive, then it is possible). The Agent then told us that they cancelled all the training scheduled for the ranges in and around this area (from the one we were at to about three back and two north if that makes sense, so about six total). He then went on to explain that they would be investigating the sighting and determining the validity of it. They never outright said what it was we were looking for, at first, but seemed to be clear on the fact that it wasn't just a "bear" that they were out looking for. And it seemed like a lot of effort to me just for a bear sighting. We were all (meaning the regular Soldiers) thinking the same thing: Big Foot.

The 1LT got up next, and just went over our mission next, stating what our duties would be, which I found to be odd as soon as he explained that we would actually be conducting PSD style security for the Government teams. I found it kind of strange that they would need us following them around fully armed in the woods while they searched for a bear or whatever it was, and even weirder that they wanted us doing it using actual tactical movements and they had planned on doing most of this late at night and in the early morning hours using our NODS (night vision goggles). The whole thing was just odd to me once the initial briefings were over (which took about six to eight hours including a lunch break). The Operation was planned for a later date, and we were to be prepared and ready to go by that time. The Platoon Sergeant (PSG) of the group was a cool guy, and seemed to just take the whole thing in stride and kind of just take it as a joke in a way. He was making Big Foot jokes (not around the LT or any of the Government people) like the rest of us were.

We had a few more briefings like that the following weeks, and a couple more training days just to get used to working with each other as a Platoon. They seemed to want to get us used to the idea that we could very well be interacting with some kind of unknown creature and yet, never outright said it in any of those briefings. And all of my buddies in my normal unit kept asking me about the detail, but I just had to tell them that it was just some boring science thing. It was kind of an odd situation, and I just wanted to get it over with. It was planned for early October, which was nice at least, since Drum usually gets super miserable and cold by the end of the month.

Anyway, the night of the operation finally comes, and we all head over to the staging area to link up and get ready to board the trucks to head out. The PSG kind of relied on me to be the guy who goes back and forth between him and the LT because I wasn't a moron and that just meant I had even more tasks to do to get ready. It was getting chilly at night, and we had a lot of packing and prepping to do in the parking lot of HQ. We loaded up, and drove out to that same Range building parking lot. Once there, we linked back up with the Agents from the Government, and the research teams. They went over the plans as far as where we would be looking, and what the plans were in terms of what to do. I wasn't exactly a part of these talks, since I was only an E4. So I don't know what was said in any of these talks, but I'll get more into this later.

We ended up moving out not long after, once everyone was ready to go. The platoon had set up with a split team movement, meaning that we had a parameter surrounding the government team so that we could provide security on all sides of them while we went through the woods. Our LT guided the movements, with the Agents and leader of the Land Management team navigating.

I was in the back of the movement, with the Platoon Sergeant during the movements, just sort of scanning my area. I had my night vision up, since I didn't feel like I really needed it, and was just scanning back and forth. I always liked that sort of thing, it was one of the reasons I joined the Infantry, the chance to walk around in the woods and "play" Army. Even after a yearlong of fighting in Iraq and I still loved that stuff. I was enjoying myself, even when we'd stop for twenty or thirty minutes, and the Government people would do whatever it was they were doing... picking up samples, tracking, etc.

The first night went on like this until morning, around 0845 or so. We made it back to the Range Control building, tired and worn out and didn't seem to find anything too interesting. Everyone was just ready to crash and try again the next night. Since we were just there to provide security, we didn't have much to do other than clean our weapons and BS with each other during the day, while the Government people actually worked on the stuff they picked up overnight. The same thing happened the next night, as we had left at the same time, and found nothing of note, in a different path. Though, we had thought we had heard something, but it might have just been some other kind of animal.

By night three, I think our (PSG?) had figured we were just part of a big rib and wondered why we were taking this whole thing so serious. It started to rain early in the evening and was cold and pretty miserable. None of us wanted to even be out there, and nobody really thought we were actually looking for anything, because nobody believed that those guys had seen anything but a bear anyway. After all, they were just dumb Soldiers anyway. But, at around 0245 or so, we learned that we weren't just wasting our time after all. And that the Government people knew that the whole time. That's where this story becomes even harder to tell. We had come across an area of really thick bramble (I think that's what it's called, the prickly stuff) brush that had been matted down in some areas and pulled up around in others. It looked like something had made some sort of shelter out of it, and used it to keep things out of the area in a way. The research people took some photos of it, and looked around for some samples and we were there for maybe twenty minutes. Then we started to head back out... again, I was in the rear of the formation.

About three or four minutes after we started back off walking, the sound of gun fire erupted in the woods. It was a sound I hadn't been startled by since Iraq, and wasn't expecting to hear at all on this detail, even though they told us it might have been part of our assignment. Our training kicked in, and we all got down on a knee and quickly scanned our area, we heard yelling, and cease fire. Then I heard someone yelling for our Medic to come forward. Our Platoon Sergeant went up with him. I stayed in the back and continued to pull security. There were maybe six to ten shots in rapid succession total, if that. Our nerves and adrenaline were on edge, and I just remember looking back and forth to the other couple guys in the back of the group and sort of just shrugging and wondering just what the heck had happened up there.

After a long, unknown, our PSG finally comes back and says to us something along the lines of "You're not going to f***-ing believe it. They just shot and killed something big up there, something not human." I still wasn't sure what he was talking about, and asked him pretty much that. And he had this baffled look on his face, and just said something like "I don't know, just go look." So, I got up, and went up towards the front of the formation to where most of the Government people and the PL (Platoon Leader; Lieutenant) were at. They had their flood light out and the Medic had her Aid Bag out and opens on the ground. I saw (right away) something huge and dark on the ground in the middle of them. Steam was coming off of it, lots of steam. That's the one thing I'll probably never forget from that night.

My eyes were probably the size of dinner plates, and I remember saying "What is that?!" Somebody from the Government team said "It's an illusory hominid. They're more common than you realize, but not nearly as many as there used to be." Or something like that. I just remember that term "elusory hominid, as it would come up many times after that. That is apparently the term used for the creature by that specific team, though could be that agency, again I'm only speaking on what I know from this operation. I got closer, and looked down. The animal (or creature, or whatever you'd like to call it) was lying in a slumped over position, in a familiar position to someone who had just been shot. It was a common pose that I was used to seeing. It happens when someone is lunging or running and is shot. They tend to "crumple" over like that. It was clearly a male, as it had male genitals visible from behind its legs, and it had that long, course hair that I guess a lot of people who see these kinds of creatures would agree they tend to have. It was night, so at the time, the hair appeared to be rather dark, but seeing the animal later in the morning, it was more of a brown color.

It had noticeable twigs, leaves, and other things caught up in the hair as if it had been running through the trees, which may have been from when it was lunging at the front of the team and not from its normal routine... hard to say, as I wasn't an expert. I couldn't see its face, since it was face down at the time, but I could see a lot of dark blood pooling in the dirt from that area, and from around its chest. Its hands and arms were up underneath its chest, as though maybe it grabbed its chest when first shot instead of trying to brace the fall. I remember the bottom of the feet were very white compared the rest of the body, and stood out, and one of the feet were up in the air because of the position of the body and the way it fell.

I couldn't take my eyes off the body, just like I seemed to always have a problem with in Iraq. Something about the reality of death always affected me that way, and I always had an odd feeling being confronted with it. Added with the fact that I was being presented with the hard truth of something that "wasn't supposed to be real" all of sudden, and it was a very surreal and strange moment. I also remember hearing a few of the Government people arguing and talking about whether or not they should continue looking for more, or if they should just wrap it up and take this one back and consider it taken care of for now. I asked one of the Infantry guys up from who shot him, and one of the Team Leaders said that they think they all probably got a couple shots off. It surprised the crap out of them and came out of nowhere, and said they didn't even see it or hear it until it was just about on top of them.

I ended up going back to the back of the formation while the Government people took pictures, samples, and did more of whatever else they do, and we were there another hour or so. Finally, we got ready to move out again. They had gotten a body bag out, and volunteered some guys to carry the animal back to the Range building. I remember watching as they tried to fit the animal inside of the bag, it was a normal size body bag, and this thing was probably over 7 feet tall and probably a few hundred pounds, and dead weight. They wrestled with it and finally got in it, and had to drag it back through the deep woods and mud. We traded out a few times, but since I was carrying an M249 (machine gun) I never had to actually carry it, thankfully. By the time we made it back, the guys who did, looked pretty much smoked and covered in mud. It was getting light out, and the rain had stopped by this point at least. I had noticed that one of the Government trucks that had been there before had been prepped and ready to go; it was a large silver semi-truck with white cab. They had the guys carrying the animal stop and open the bag back up, that's when we all got another look at it. They had them pull the animal back out and the Government people took some more pictures, this time of the face, the hands and feet, and the bullet wounds. They added some tags to the lips and nose. It looked a lot like those old cave man people but also kind of like a monkey or ape, but just huge. Again, it's probably cliché to say it, but it really does look like what a lot of people who say they see them say they look like.

Our PL kind of rushed us away from it though, and didn't seem to want us standing around and looking at it, and didn't want us to even really talk about it. We had to go inside of the building and start our usual weapons cleaning and after-action stuff. None of us were as tired, because of the curiosity of the situation. We all were on edge and excited because of what had happened and wondered what was next. We had no idea what we had just found and wondered if we were going to be famous now for having discovered a new creature, being the first to discover Sasquatch. Our PL told us just to shut up about it, and told us to remember our mission and that we're not supposed to talk about it at all until we know more for sure. By the time we had everything all cleaned and done, and got back outside, the silver semi-truck was already gone, and some of the government people were gone. The body was gone too.

The PL talked with the Fish and Wildlife Agent and CID Agent and some of the other people, and we were told just to go ahead with the rest of the OPORD plan and wrap things up. They would take care of everything else, and he again stressed to keep things on the hush and hush. So we packed everything up, loaded up the trucks, and headed back to the Brigaded HQs. As I mentioned before, the PSG kind of had me doing a lot of the back and forth with the PL, so I had a copy of the OPORD and knew was all the steps were and knew what was involved as far as downturn. We turned our weapons back in, turned the trucks back in to the motor-pools, and were released for the remainder of the next week while they worked on the After Action Report and the debriefing.

This happened the following week, at the same Range building. It'd be the last time we all (meaning the Platoon detail and the Government people) would be working together. They stressed how good of a job we did, how professional everyone was, how exciting it was to have been successful in the operation, and again how we all needed to abide by the security clearance keep quite on the matter. It was vital on this point because of reasons that we weren't to be included on, but that we needed to understand were important to the security of the United States and the population. At the time, I just figured that as the usual case of "You don't need to know because you're just dumb Infantrymen." which was probably true. Take it for whatever you will, I don't know. We also went over the final AAR, which was now being called OPERATION CLOUDED MOHAWK (I guess because of the Natives in that area). An AAR is an After Action Report and just goes over the basics of "what the plan was; what you were trying to do; what you did; what the outcome was; and what you could have done better." We all got a handshake and some other perks I won't mention, and went back to main post after that final meeting.

The LT had me make some copies for him at the Brigade HQ because he would be sending off reports of the AAR to whomever, that's where I come into play in all of this, as I mentioned earlier. I was sort of the middle man because I wasn't dumb. I spent that entire week after that night we killed that animal thinking about it and wondering what it was, how smart it was, how it lived, why it was there, and why we did what we did. And I didn't like the way it was treated after we encountered it. The whole thing just seemed weird and I didn't like it, so I felt like maybe I should make copies for myself, so that I'll at least be able to remember the details of it. So, since I was sitting in the empty S-shop of the Brigade building making copies for the LT, I made copies of the AAR and all the other paperwork for myself and left them in the printer. I came back out, and handed him his copies. After I said my final goodbyes to the guy, I went back into the office, picked up the stack of papers, and put them in a black manila folder and got out of there.

I've had that folder ever since buried away with all of my other Army paperwork. I have tried to just sit on it and forget about it, but like I said, it hasn't really been easy and it's something that just always seems to stand out and bother me. And lately, the Government has been giving me good reason on a personal level to want to not exactly be quiet anymore about it at all. I can't say for sure whether or not I'll ever release the entire AAR (which has the complete report, in detail of the event, include many things I haven't mentioned) but who knows, maybe I will. I don't want to get in trouble, and maybe I will anyway, but sometimes you reach a point where the truth matters more.

I eventually left Fort Drum and became an Instructor at Fort Benning at the Javelin School, served a couple more years before having to get out because of complications from my injury in Iraq. I served honorably and don't want people to think that any of this is me bashing the Army; this isn't what this is about at all. I loved my time in the Army; I just also love the truth, and served with a code of conduct and values that included Integrity and honesty. I realize now that many people are seeking the truth in this subject and many people want validity when it comes to these "elusory hominids" and I am now willing to risk bringing that truth to the forefront. I'm including my discharge papers, my state ID, and the appointment orders for now. I (As you'll see, the First and Last name's match up, the birthdates match up, the States and address of record match up, and the time frames match up to prove that I am who I say I am, and my service is the correct time frame. Without giving out too much information, so I hope to stay somewhat in secret to protect myself as much as I can give the information I've told in this thread. I only blacked out what I felt I needed to in order to protect myself.) Maybe I'll add more, who knows.

I'm surprised I've even said this much honestly. Forgive me if I've left things out, there is just only so much I can or am willing to say, maybe will change. I'll be willing to answer questions, though I can't say how much of an answer I will be able to give on all questions.

I apologize for the length of this, and I am sure plenty of you may have your doubts, which is perfectly understandable, but I am only (here) to tell my story and offer it to those who want to know the truth in this incident. I want to provide as much info as I can, without placing too much of my neck out there, if that makes sense.

32 PAM'S ENCOUNTER

I have spent a long time getting this down on paper and I have to say I feel immensely relieved to have "got it off my chest" so to speak!

At the time of the event, the 3 of us would talk about it sporadically for the first few days but afterwards never brought it up. My brother was too weirded out by it and my husband was in total disbelief, and shock. When the subject came up they both shut it down fast and got very emotional. I swore (we made a pact) I'd never talk about it to others; folks' think we were druggies and he had respectable job at risk; my brother was excelling at school.

After 42 years, I have started to recall the event more and more, especially since seeing so much about Sasquatch etc. on TV and the web. I really started researching the subject about 5 yrs. ago after I made the connection that the creature we saw may have been a type of Sasquatch! All these years I thought we had seen something no one else had reported.....

My brother only barely acknowledges the account when I talk to him about it (last time was over 10 yrs. ago) and my now, ex-husband, never spoke of it.

I told my daughter and present husband this account just last year, and they were astounded that I had kept a secret of it. My husband is creeped out and gets very nervous if I talk about it and when I have a you tube video on with Bigfoot related things he tears out of the room. So I have been pretty isolated and quiet about this whole ordeal. I began to realize I was not crazy and did experience a cryptid sighting- just not your run of the mill Bigfoot!

I thank you sincerely for the time you are taking to read all this, and maybe have a little more information on the type of animal we saw. I know one thing for sure; I am so much more relieved after hearing others' tales of odd and menacing creatures in our forests.

It was Oct. 1972 when my 20 yr. old husband, our two baby's age 14 mos. and 2 mos., my brother Bruce age 16 and I, age 18 left Leavenworth, KS on a camping trip to Arkansas. We'd visited the Beaver Lake project twice before on day trips, and since the reservoir had been filling since completion in 1966, we expected it to be ready for full use and campsites all completed.

We found a fairly remote campsite at the far end of the park with only 4 sites and located at the end of a high rock ridge line. We wanted to be alone as the babies woke often at night and needed feeding etc. and didn't want to wake any other campers. My brother pitched a pup tent by the fire pit for his digs and we were going to be in our 1968 VW van at night. Babies on the back over-the-engine compartment ledge in back, me on the back seat and hubby on the floor behind the front seats. The van had the 2 side doors that opened
Outward, on the passenger side.

The campsite was in an area with a horseshoe shaped rocky, terraced ledge rising from 50' to around 100' as it curved behind the 4 sites. Brush and small deciduous trees ran up its sides and the top was covered in mature trees and brush so thick daylight had trouble poking into our little spot. Our site's campfire ring was about 10' from the left side of the rock wall and wispy shrubs separated the site from the rock wall base.

Next to our site was a site with a line of small trees and bushes between us and it was lower than our site so we looked down onto the roof of their pickup when they pulled in. It was around 30-40' away from us and downslope, and was basically on the road into the camp area. The other sites were back against the rock ledge behind us (60' approx.) and far to the right end of the curved rock wall (around 100' away). And were empty. We were told by the ranger station we were the very first customers to ever use the new camping area.

It was rainy and grey and during sunbreaks, quite hot out. The dam reservoir had a swimming area and my husband and brother decided to swim during a particularly hot sunbreak, not knowing that all the recent rain and area flooding had caused a very strong undercurrent. My brother came back to shore quickly and said he had trouble just swimming back after going out only a short distance- so we called to my husband who'd ventured even farther out. Yelling for him to come back didn't reach him so I honked the van horn and he turned to shore. After an agonizingly long fight to get to land he gave up and went under! My brother was able to go out far enough with a tree branch to drag him in and pull him onto the shore....my husband was virtually drowned...he was blue and we CPR'd him till he coughed and puked. Racing to the Ranger station we got directions to Rogers, AR where they had a small hospital. Long story short- he had pneumonia, should stay overnight (we had insurance) but he wouldn't!

So off to our campsite we went. We were told to watch him for 48 hrs. - Plenty of sleep etc. So Bruce and I would sleep in shifts and check him all night. It was around suppertime when we got there so we made sandwiches and beans on the campfire as husband passed out on the van floor. He shivered, and sweat and slept deeply. About that time a pickup truck with a small pop up tent trailer came into set up camp next to us in the site I mentioned above. A family of 4 was done eating and as darkness fell we too were turning in- me on backseat of the van and my brother Bruce into his pup tent by the fire embers. A long and frightening day was going to get a little scarier.

Bruce took 2nd shift checking on Husband so at 11 pm he opened the van passenger door, got in and I nodded off to much needed sleep. When the 2 mo. old woke at 3 for feeding I relieved Bruce and he went to the tent.
At around 3:30 a.m. I heard some animal sounds on the ridge-coyotes? The babes were asleep and all was quiet...I looked out the window at the lower campsite and it was dark; the fire pit was dark and

out. Still hearing odd yips and howls I was edgy but lay back down with my head at the passenger door side of the back seat van wall. BANG!!!! Suddenly a huge loud crashing BANG reverberated off the van side wall right by my head! I pictured a huge softball thrown at 100 miles an hour at the van....my husband leapt up out of full sleep-my brother bolted into the van from the pup tent outside and a whole lot of panic hit. Husband yelled what the hell? And Bruce was looking out the front seat window, I out the side where it came from and husband was looking all over too. Bruce then yelled that he saw something moving in the rearview mirror! We all looked out the back window...a large shadow passed about 20' behind the back of the van heading down to the other campsite!!!

The kids were fussing and I immediately got them silenced and kept my head low- scared spitless. We then saw that the people in the pop up camper were moving about folding it down and getting kids into truck. Just a flashlight some words and they were out of there in less than 10 minutes leaving the trailer behind and peeled out!

Husband and brother decided it must be ok to go out and see what hit the van and there was not even a mark on it! Impossibly, not a scratch or dent...nada.
They were saying that maybe there was a hillbilly that was mad about the Park
Being open now and wanted to freak us out of there (?) and trying to make sense of what was happening. Now being about 20 minutes. after the

initial BANG- people left and us scratching our heads - walking sounds - pounding steps- came from the brush at the rock ledge behind our van around 50' away!

It sounded like King Kong was walking down a flight of stairs- you could tell it was coming down the rock ledge in steps! It was moving in an arc from left to right of us and behind us...we froze. The guys eased into the front seats of the van from the open back doors beside me and I closed them ever so gingerly. Not a sound. Then, all of a sudden my husband turned the headlights on and punched the brakes for rear light! At once- there was a massive scuffling and breaking twigs, rocks falling behind and beside us!! He started the van up and in the glow around us, of the lighting shed by headlights, off to the _front right_ side of the van -1/2 way up the ridge and only 10' away from us a hairy thing was coming down in steps off the ridge! As it got closer the hair glistened at the ends silver tipped, with a greyish streak from shoulders down the back to its buttocks. It was head down and went from standing stepping to 4 legs crawling as it descended the ridge! I saw only glimpses of facial features-slim lips; hairless cheeks; boxy short snout (?) or flattish square nose; hair on the head was about 2-4" and longer off the arms.

The body hair seemed darker and got more silver tipped as it reached the shoulders, and the back was then totally grey in center. It was around 7-8' - unsure as it stood/crawled so much, and had a barrel shaped chest and slim legs. He never looked up enough for a true view of the eyes etc. but I saw enough that the face was not ape like...had ears with tufts of fur at tops, was very humanlike in movements and general body . He was moving smoothly and quickly and in 3 minutes. Or so he was at the brush line of the Rockledge, 15' from the back rt. of the van and stood and walked around the back of the van following the base of the ridge! It let out a menacing "Huff! 'And low rumbling growls like a dog...

Insanely, my brother and husband bolted from the van (?!) and tried to get a better look! They cowered at the front of the van blocking headlights a bit, and I lost sight due to the lack of light. They were asking each other "what do you see?" "Where is it?" etc., when a shower of gravel came at us! If I had to estimate, I'd say it was like a small laundry basket full was tossed in one fell swoop! A literal hail storm of rock! They guys were in the van so fast and we were burning up the road getting out of there. I kept looking out the back window and they used the rear view mirrors but we never saw it.

We didn't stop till we exited the park and saw a small store where we parked for the rest of the night- under their streetlight. I asked what they saw- they asked what I saw and we talked for a hr. before my husband succumbed to the pneumonia and passed out. My brother said it had to be a bear, a deformed German shepherd (what? 7'tall) or maybe an inbred hillbilly. I kept saying but it walked upright, it had hands to throw such a huge weighty amount of rock at us- but it had such weird hair etc. We fell asleep around 5:00 am exhausted.

At 6 am when the store was opening I awoke to feed the babes. I went inside and there was a man and woman working to open the store. I got a few items and as I paid I asked them if they had reports of anything unusual. Like weird animals, bears that walk upright a lot....they looked at me like I was crazy.
I was wreck I am sure, and looked the part. The woman said "Mebbe you saw the White River monster huh?" and they both laughed. I left.

I pulled into the ranger station and told him we were leaving 3 days early...and about the incident. He was big eyed and listened intently, but said he was there from some other state actually- and had not heard of such a thing. He was going to go up and check out the site and we said just keep the pup tent and sleeping bag!

Driving back to Leavenworth, my brother and I hypothesized everything you could dream of. We fell silent after a while and when husband awoke him and Bruce made up the "pact" and I signed on. My brother was finishing high school early, as I had, and had a school for veterinary science picked out and didn't want anything to ruin that. We were raised in the Army by a Staff sgt. and a homemaker- poor as heck. Travelled the world- grew up smarter because of it. Dad was a drill instructor during Viet Nam era, a Korean War wounded vet, a merchant marine at 15 and an all- around mean sob. that taught us how to survive in the woods by living it. When he retired our family spent 6 mos. living off the land Near Quantico Marine Base VA....just because he could. We had a huge Army tent and tools, a station wagon and guts. Looking back now, I wouldn't trade that time for all the money in the world.

When I asked Dad about the incident, 30 yrs. later - if Bruce had mentioned it to him, he said a bit. He said he knew it was a bad campout etc. and asked what happened. Bruce told him about hearing a very large creature and the rock throwing but was very cool about it etc. Dad said he was told growing up in logging camps around Mt Rainier (especially Mineral, WA) and being from Tacoma, that they were never ever to go out into the tree line or woods alone as the "boss of the woods" or "Old man of the woods" could take you as a slave or eat you! He said the men working the camps would tell stories and he told me some.

  It just didn't sound like Sasquatch was what we had encountered. It seemed more dog-like in the face; too slim in the body type.
I started to make a connection between the several types of Sasquatch there may be, and the rock throwing menacing behavior we experienced WAS Sasquatch like.

I still have PTSD like feelings and to this day though I am and always have been an avid outdoorswoman- I watch how and where I camp; I always zip up tent windows, and I still live in a rural Cascades wilderness where I know they are out there. I hate windows at night as I just feel their

presence (crazy I know) so I close the blinds tight at night. And yet, I am compelled to learn more and want to see pictures etc. reports about them.
If you have heard of another creature like this (dog man?) or account similar I'd appreciate hearing/reading it.   42 yrs. and I still look for an answer or even a glimpse of what that was.

33 "Q"

The incident happened around early spring. During this time the sasquatches other than watching us, and occasionally prowling around the place at night weren't going out of their way to bother us.

 It was late afternoon the sun was going down, and I want to say it was after, or around 5pm on a warm day. The sun was still setting fairly early around that time of year. My mom lived alone, and I would tend to her two dogs while she traveled for work. That day was a quiet one; I let the dogs go outside for a little while, and after putting them back in the house. I'd gotten in my car, and drove to the entrance gate of the property. There were always deer around, to see them grazing wasn't uncommon. As I got ready to pull out I noticed a deer on the property across from my Mom's house. I watched the deer for just a few seconds, and didn't think too much of it. Then saw a black streak emerge from the brush. There was a patch of brush the Male would often use to hide behind, and in, after he crossed the road on my Mom's side of the land. Out of nowhere the Male ran out of the brush patch, he was crouched down because I saw him rise, then run. And he moved so quickly the deer didn't see him coming. His gate when he ran reminded me of two gears, the legs were moving lightning fast. His arms did swing as he ran but were moving as if he were almost casually jogging. The deer wasn't that far away from him. The deer didn't have a clue what was about to happen to him. It didn't move, or react, or flee, and I don't think it would've had a chance had it seen the male due to how quickly it descended upon it. The male covered that ground so quickly it was mind blowing. It grabbed the deer with both hands, the left hand grabbed the front of the deer, and the right hand grabbed the tail end of the deer's back. The Male snatched it off the ground to about the creatures chest level, viciously slammed the deer full force on the ground upon its neck, and chest region. This seemed to paralyze the deer. I could tell it was still alive. It then picked the deer up, and put it over its right shoulder, and quickly walked into the tree line that was about 15 feet away from it. It took the male less than 30 seconds to take that deer down. The male never even so much as looked in my direction, but he had to have known I was there, and had to have seen me getting ready to exit the property.

34 THE BAUMAN INCIDENT

"Frontiersmen are not, as a rule, apt to be very superstitious. They lead lives too hard and practical, and have too little imagination in things spiritual and supernatural. I have heard but a few ghost stories while living on the frontier and those few were of a perfectly commonplace type.

But I once listened to a goblin story, which rather impressed me. It was told by a grizzled, weather beaten old mountain hunter, named Bauman, who was born and had passed all of his life on the frontier. He must have believed what he said, for he could hardly repress a shudder at certain points of the tale; but he was of German ancestry; and in childhood had doubtless been saturated with all kinds of ghost and goblin lore, so that many fearsome superstitions were latent in his mind; besides, he knew well the stories told by the Indian medicine men in their winter camps, of the snow walkers, and the specters, and the lonely formless evil beings that haunt the forest depths, and dog and waylay the lonely wanderer who after nightfall passes through the regions where they lurk; and it may be that when overcome by the horror of the fate that befell his friend, and when oppressed by the awful dread of the unknown, he grew to attribute, both at the time and in remembrance, weird and elf in traits to what was merely some abnormally, weird wicked wild beast; but whether this was so or not, no man can say.

When the event occurred, Bauman was still a young man, and was trapping with a partner among the mountains dividing the forks of the Salmon from the head of the Wisdom River. Not having had much luck, he and his partner determined to go up into a particularly wild and lonely pass through which ran a small stream said to contain many beaver. The pass had an evil reputation because the year before a solitary hunter who had wandered into it was there slain by a wild beast, the half-eaten remains being afterwards found by some mining prospectors who had passed his camp only the night before.

The memory of this event, however, weighed very lightly with the two trappers, who were as adventurous and hardy as others of their kind. They took their two lean mountain ponies to the foot of the pass where they left them in an open beaver meadow, the rocky timber clad ground being from there onward impracticable for horses. They then struck out on foot through the vast, gloomy forest, and in about four hours reached a little open glade where they concluded to camp, as signs of game were plenty.

There was still about an hour of daylight left, and after building a brush lean-to and throwing down and opening their packs, they started upstream. The country was very dense and hard to travel through, as there was much down timber, although here and there the somber woodland was broken by small glades of mountain grass. At dusk they again reached camp. The glade in which it was pitched was not many yards wide, the tall close-set pines and firs rising round it like a wall. On one side was a little stream, beyond which rose the steep mountain slope, covered with the unbroken growth of evergreen forest.

They were surprised to find that during their absence something, apparently a bear, had visited camp, and had rummaged about their things, scattering the contents of their packs, and in sheer wantonness destroying their lean-to. The footprints were quite plain, but at they first paid no particular heed to them, busying themselves with rebuilding the lean-to, laying out their beds and stores and lighting the fire.

While Bauman was making ready supper, it being already dark, his companion began to examine the tracks more closely, and soon took a brand from the fire to follow them up, where the intruder walked along a game trail after leaving camp. When the brand flickered out, he returned and took another, repeating his inspection of the footprints very closely. Coming back to the fire, he stood by it a minute or two, peering out into the darkness, and suddenly remarked, "Bauman, that bear has been walking on two legs." Bauman laughed at this, but his partner insisted that he was right, and upon again examining the tracks with a torch, they certainly did seem to be made but by two paws or feet. However, it was too dark to make sure. After discussing whether the footprints could possibly be those of a human being, and coming to the conclusion that they couldn't be, the two men rolled up in their blankets and went to sleep under the lean-to.

At midnight Bauman was awakened by some noise, and sat up in his blankets. As he did so his nostrils were struck by a strong, wild beast odor, and he caught the loom of a great body in the darkness at the mouth of the lean-to. Grasping his rifle, he fired at the vague, threatening shadow, but must have missed, for immediately afterwards he heard the smashing of the underwood as the thing, whatever it was, rushed off into the impenetrable blackness of the forest and the night.

After this the two men slept but little, sitting up by the rekindled fire, but they heard nothing more. In the morning they started out to look at the few traps they had set the previous evening and put out new ones. By an unspoken agreement they kept together all day, and returning to camp towards evening.

On returning they saw, hardly to their astonishment, that the lean-to had again been torn down. The visitor of the preceding day had returned, and in wanton malice had tossed about their camp kit and bedding, and destroying the shanty. The ground was marked up by its tracks, and on leaving the camp it had gone along the soft earth by the brook, where the footprints were as plain as if on snow, and, after careful scrutiny of the trail, it certainly did seem as if, whatever the thing was, it had walked off on but two legs.

The men, thoroughly uneasy, gathered a great heap of logs and kept up a roaring fire throughout the night, one or the other sitting on guard most of the time. About midnight the thing came down through the forest opposite, across the brook, and stayed there on the hillside for nearly an hour. They could hear the branches crackle as it moved about, and several times it uttered a harsh, grating, long drawn moan, a particularly sinister sound. Yet it didn't venture near the fire.

In the morning the two trappers, after discussing the strange events of the last 36 hours, decided that they would shoulder their packs and leave the valley that afternoon. They were more ready to do this in spite of seeing a good deal of game sign they had caught very little fur. However it was necessary first to go along their line of their traps and gather them, and this they started to do. All morning they kept together, picking up trap after trap, each one being empty. On first leaving camp they had the disagreeable sensation of being followed. In the dense spruce thickets they occasionally heard a branch snap after that had been passed; and now and then there were slight rustling noises among the small pines to one side of them.

At noon they were back within a couple miles of camp. In the high, bright sunlight their fears seemed absurd to the two armed men, accustomed as they were, through long years of lonely wandering in the wilderness, to face every kind of danger from man, brute or element. There were still three beaver traps to collect from a little pond in a wide ravine nearby. Bauman volunteered to gather these and bring them in, while his companion went and made ready the packs.

On reaching the pond, Bauman found three beavers in the traps, one of which had been pulled loose and carried into the beaver house. He took several hours in securing and preparing the beaver, and when he started homewards he marked, with some uneasiness, how low the sun was getting. As he hurried toward camp, under the small trees, the silence and desolation of the forest weighed on him. His feet made no sound on the pine needles and the slanting sunrays, striking through among the strait trunks, made a gray twilight in which objects at a distance glimmered indistinctly. There was nothing to break the gloomy stillness whish, when there is no breeze, always broods over those somber primeval forests.

At last he came to the edge of the little glade where the camp lay, and shouted as he approached it, but got no answer to his call. The campfire had gone out, though the thin blue smoke was still curling upwards.

Near it laid the packs, wrapped and arranged. At first Bauman could see nobody; nor did he receive an answer to his call. Stepping forward he again shouted, and as he did so his eye fell on the body of his friend. Stretched beside the trunk of a great fallen spruce. Rushing towards it the horrified trapper found that the body was still warm, but that the neck was broken, while there were four great fang marks in the throat.

The footprints of the unknown beast-creature, printed the soft soil, told the whole story.

The unfortunate man, having finished packing, had sat down on the spruce log with his face to the fire, and his back to the dense woods, to wait for his companion. While thus waiting, his monstrous assailant, who must have been lurking in the woods, waited for a chance to catch one of the adventurers unprepared, came silently up from behind, walking still on two legs. Evidently unheard, it reached the man, and broke his neck by wrenching his head back with its forepaws, while buried its teeth in his throat. It had not eaten the body, but apparently had romped and gamboled around it in uncouth, ferocious glee, occasionally rolling over and over it, and had fled back into the soundless depths of the woods.

Bauman, utterly unnerved, and believing that the creature with which he had to deal was something either half human or half devil, some great goblin-beast, abandoned everything but his rifle struck off at speed down the pass, not halting until he reached the beaver meadows where the hobbled ponies were still grazing. Mounting, he rode onwards through the night, until beyond the reach of pursuit."

35 NARROW ESCAPE

Jackson County, Prospect, Oregon (Union Creek) 2001....

Back in the winter of 2001 my youngest son and I were on our way from Boise Idaho to Medford Oregon.

We had taken a car trailer to his old place in Boise in order to haul his non-running Jeep to his new place in
 Medford. We hit an area of heavy snow in the southern Cascades around 2:00 a.m. It took 45 minutes or so to get down the mountain. We had of course been drinking coffee to stay alert.

About 25 miles west of the pass it became obvious that the last few quarts of coffee had to be drained. We stopped at a wide spot in the road near a summer tourist haunt; deserted in winter. There is a gas station and ice cream joint on the west side of the road, closed this time of year and no town or settlement within 30 miles.

This is tall timber country and unsettled. Across the road is a small parking area for the ice cream joint. It is paved and about 200 ft. wide and 80 ft. deep. I pulled in and as I stepped out with .45 on hip, it occurred to me in a flash that grabbing the 590 Mossy would be good.

As we walked to the far end of the area to be well off the road, the hair on my arms and the back of my neck stood on end. The area directly to our front was open with a depth of 50 yards and a width of 100 yards. The night was clear and cold, 8-10 inches of snow on the ground and with a moon almost full, so we could see quite well. *While standing and taking a leak with son about 15 ft. to my right I saw, as if springing from the earth in front of us across the open area 10 or 12 creatures moving RAPIDLY back and forth in sort of a Thatch weave pattern.*
These things, not human men, were close to 7 ft. tall, thin, bipedal with long arms, medium length gray fur, and damned fast on their feet. I brought the shotgun up and slid the safety off, as son was drawing his .45.

I don't know if I can adequately explain the overwhelming feeling of menace, but here goes. I had been operating on pure instinct since I had stepped from the pickup, the rotten feeling hit me a split second before the things arrived, the feeling?, instinct?, was that we were prey and subject to a very bad death and to be slaughtered and eaten, not a logical process, gut feeling and massively overwhelming.

As they were moving around in front of us, more appeared and mixed among them, all the while running about fast in front of us. Son and I were backing toward the truck, I WOULD NOT present my back to them and *some of them peeled off right and left in an encirclement movement. They were rolling in fast from the sides now; I could smell and feel their presence.*

We got to the truck loaded on adrenaline and ready to kill, as we both knew we were in grave danger. We piled into the truck, locked doors. I had keys out and ready as my butt neared the seat, I had the engine lit and trans. in gear and gas pedal mashed in one motion. Adrenaline is great stuff! As we fled, yes fled, *something VERY close by let out an undulating scream of rage, and pain. I believe one or more of the group had gotten really close to us in their pursuit and I ran over the foot of one of them,* yeah they were that close.

We rolled onto the highway and I told son to watch the bed of the pickup as well as the trailer, he already was indexed to the rear with the shotgun. We hauled ass for at least 20 miles before the feeling of grave danger started to abate. The feeling that nailed both of us as we discussed soon afterward, was one of being prey and soon to be slaughtered and eaten. I am not easily led and neither believe or disbelieve all the Bigfoot, ghost and werewolf stuff, in fact I am skeptical.

Son was speaking with a coworker about 6 months later who had grown up in Prospect, Oregon, about 30 miles south of Union Creek where the incident took place. He asked Jake if he had ever heard of any strange goings-on in the area. Jake went ashy white and pretty much retold the above tale. He says to avoid the place at night.

A family friend, a 25 yr. retired cop not given to flights of fancy and an excellent observer, had a tale very similar from a year before. I told my wife of this event of course; she looked at me at the beginning as though I had developed a 3rd eyeball in the center of my forehead. That was from shock, she did believe me, but did not wish to hear any details. She said the tale gave her chills. Me too, as I write this, hair on back of neck and forearms is sticking up.

I have NOT gone back to explore and would not without a large group of shotgun and flamethrower equipped men with me. Son and I are both sane, sober persons, and not taken to hysteria. We were wide, VERY wide awake as things transpired.
We saw and smelled what was there.

As a sidebar neither of us heard footfalls from the creatures. They were silent until I heard one as we were getting the hell out of there.

To my knowledge, and I have researched, there is nothing that matches these creatures, unless one considers old legends and folk tales of were creatures.

To conclude, I have to fall back on Elmer Keith's famous line,
Hell, I was there.

ABOUT THE AUTHOR

William Jevning is a two time witness of the Sasquatch, author of Notes From the Field, Tracking North Americas Sasquatch, In Search of the Unknown, Haunted Valley, The Minnesota Iceman and Bigfoot Field Work 101. Participant on the TV show Americas Book of Secrets, the mystery of Bigfoot and numerous radio shows and podcasts. Website is williamjevning.com